More Praise for *The Servant*

"An engaging story that takes the reader right to the heart of leadership! This puts character back into the discussion of leadership style."
**—Bill Thatcher, President,
The Foundation for Community Encouragement**

"A deftly drawn reminder that effective leadership is based upon service to others and a heedlessness of self."
—James M. Strock, author of *Reagan on Leadership*

"*The Servant* tells us how we need to act and who we need to be like. It provokes thoughtfulness as you read it. Add this to your library if you care about people."
—Rob Lebow, founder of the Shared Values Process operating system and author of *Journey into the Heroic Environment*

"More often than not it is taken for granted. Whether you are chosen for the local neighborhood association or elected to Congress, before you can lead—you must serve."
**—John Boehner, Chairman, Republican Conference,
*U.S. House of Representatives***

The Servant

THE
SERVANT

*A Simple Story
About the True Essence
of Leadership*

J A M E S   C .   H U N T E R

CROWN
BUSINESS
NEW YORK

Published by Crown Business, New York, New York.
Member of the Crown Publishing Group, a division of Random House, Inc.
www.crownpublishing.com

CROWN BUSINESS and colophon are trademarks of Random House, Inc.

Originally published by Prima Publishing, Roseville, California, in 1998.

Extract from *Man's Search for Meaning* by Viktor Frankl reprinted by permission of Beacon Press, Boston, Massachusetts.

Printed in the United States of America

Library of Congress Cataloging-in-Publication Data

Hunter, James C.
   The servant : a simple story about the true essence of leadership / James C. Hunter.
      p.   cm.
      1. Leadership. 2. Leadership—Moral and ethical aspects.
I. Title.
   HD57.7.H875 1998   98-4864
   303.3'4—dc21   CIP

ISBN 0-7615-1369-8

20

First Edition

To the Glory of God

Contents

Acknowledgments   ix

The Prologue   1

CHAPTER ONE
The Definitions   15

CHAPTER TWO
The Old Paradigm   47

CHAPTER THREE
The Model   71

CHAPTER FOUR
The Verb   91

CHAPTER FIVE
The Environment   127

CHAPTER SIX
The Choice   147

CHAPTER SEVEN
The Payoff   169

The Epilogue   185

Acknowledgments

Of course, this work would not have been possible without the help of a number of people. My heartfelt thanks go out . . .

- To my first business mentor, Phil Hoffman, who taught me that being the boss and being a gentleman are not mutually exclusive roles.
- To my business associates and clients who have taught me valuable lessons over the years, especially Kevin Alder, Ed Danner, Russ Ebeid, Greg Goodman, Mike Hipsher, Mike Panther, and George Treglown.
- To authors Tony Campolo and M. Scott Peck for their skills in articulating some of the great truths of life.
- To Debra Venzke and Steve Martin at Prima for their skills and assistance throughout the editing process, and to Paula Munier Lee for her guidance and especially for her vision in recognizing the importance of the theme contained herein.
- To Simeon, monk and archabbey librarian, St. Meinrad Monastery, St. Meinrad, Indiana, for sharing "the ropes" of the monastic life with me.

• To my editors and cheerleaders, including Eric Bacon, Phyllis and Jack Hunter (my parents), Karen and Mark Jolley, Pam and Mickey Krieger, Elizabeth Morin, Karen and Bill Rajki, Colleen and Craig Ramquist, John Riley, Patty and Scott Simonson, and especially Theresa and John Vella, whose ideas and encouragement were invaluable to me.

• To my precious little girl Rachael (well into her Terrific Two's) who has been a blessing (literally) to me beyond words.

• And finally, to my life partner Denise, for her love and commitment (especially when I'm difficult to be around) as we journey together on our paths of spiritual growth. I love you, honey.

The Servant

The Prologue

The ideas I stand for are not my own. I borrowed them from Socrates, I swiped them from Chesterfield, I stole them from Jesus. And if you don't like their ideas, whose ideas would you rather use? —DALE CARNEGIE

I MADE THE CHOICE TO GO. There was no one else to blame.

As I look back at it now, I find it nearly impossible to believe that I—a busy general manager of a large manufacturing facility—left the plant to look after itself while I spent a week in a monastery in northern Michigan. Yes, that's right. A monastery. Complete with monks, five chapel services a day, chanting, liturgies, communion, shared living quarters, the whole nine yards.

Please understand, I fought it kicking and screaming.

But in the end, I made the choice to go.

"SIMEON" WAS A NAME that had haunted me from my birth.

As an infant, I was baptized at the local Lutheran church. The baptismal record showed that the Bible

1

verse selected for the ceremony was from the second chapter of Luke about some guy named Simeon. According to Luke, Simeon was a "very righteous and devout man, full of the Holy Spirit." Apparently he had an inspiration about the coming Messiah, mumbo jumbo I never really understood. That was to be my first—but certainly not my last—encounter with Simeon.

I was confirmed in the Lutheran church at the end of the eighth grade. The pastor selected a Bible verse for each confirmation candidate, and when he came to me during the ceremony he read out loud the same section in Luke about this Simeon character. "Pretty bizarre coincidence," I remember thinking at the time.

Soon after that—and for the next twenty-five years—I had a recurring dream that I came to dread. In the dream, it is late at night and I am completely lost and running for my life through a cemetery. Although I cannot see what is chasing me, I *know* it to be evil, something wishing to do me great harm. Suddenly, a man wearing a black hooded robe steps out directly in front of me from behind a large concrete crucifix. As I crash into him, the very old man grabs me by the shoulders, looks intently into my eyes and shouts, "Find Simeon— find Simeon and listen to him!" I would always wake up at this point in a cold sweat.

To top it all off, on my wedding day the pastor referred to this biblical character Simeon during his brief homily. It stunned me to the point that I messed up reciting my vows, which was rather embarrassing.

I was never really sure if there was any meaning or significance to all of these "Simeon coincidences." My wife Rachael was always convinced that there was.

BY THE LATE 1990S, to all outward appearances, I had the world by the tail.

I was employed by a world-class flat glass manufacturer as general manager of a plant with more than five hundred employees and just over $100 million in annual sales. At the time I was promoted to the position, I was the youngest G.M. in the history of the company, a fact of which I am still very proud. My employer ran a very decentralized company allowing me great autonomy, which I relished. I had a pretty healthy salary that included significant bonus dollars provided we hit certain goals and measurables at the plant.

Rachael, my beautiful wife of eighteen years, and I first met while attending Valparaiso University in northwestern Indiana where I graduated with a business degree and she an M.A. in psychology. We desperately wanted children but struggled with infertility for several years. We did the fertility treatments, shots, tests, poking, prodding, acupuncture, you name it—all with no results. Infertility was especially hard on Rachael, but she never gave up hope of having children. I would often wake up at night and hear her quietly praying for a child.

Then, through a series of unusual but wonderful circumstances, we adopted a baby at birth and named him John (after me) and he became known as our "miracle" baby. Two years later, Rachael unexpectedly became pregnant and our second "miracle" baby, Sarah, was born.

John Jr., now fourteen, had just begun the ninth grade, Sarah the seventh. From the day we adopted John, Rachael cut back her therapy practice to just one day a week as we believed it was important, if possible, for her to be a full-time homemaker. In addition, the one day a week gave her a little break from the "mom routine" and also enabled her to keep her professional skills sharp. We were very thankful that we were able to swing it financially.

We owned (along with the bank) a very nice home on the northwest shore of Lake Erie, roughly thirty miles south of Detroit. A thirty-foot offshore-style pleasure boat was conveniently parked in a hoist behind my home (next to a Sea-Doo jet ski), we had two new leased cars in the garage, we took at least two family vacations a year, and we still managed to put a pretty good chunk of money in the bank each year for college and retirement.

As I said, to all appearances, I really did have the world by the tail.

BUT, OF COURSE, things are not always as they appear. The fact was that my life was falling apart. Rachael had told me a month earlier that she had been unhappy in the marriage for some time and insisted that things had to change. She told me that her "needs" were not being met. I could hardly believe my ears! Here I thought I was providing everything a woman could ask for and yet she said that I wasn't meeting her needs! What other needs could she possibly have?

Things with the kids were not going so well either. John Jr. was getting increasingly mouthy around the house and had even called Rachael a bitch three weeks earlier. I was so mad I nearly hit him and ended up grounding him for a week after that incident. He bucked any kind of authority or instructions from adults and even got his left ear pierced! If it hadn't been for Rachael, I would have thrown his butt right out of the house. My relationship with John Jr. had deteriorated to grunts and nods.

My relationship with my daughter Sarah also seemed to be heading south. We had always shared a special bond and I still get misty-eyed thinking of her as a little girl. But she seemed distant and even a little angry with me at times for no apparent reason. Rachael often suggested that I talk with Sarah about my feelings but I could never seem to "find the time" or, more honestly, the courage.

My work, the one area in my life where I was sure I could count on success, was also taking a turn in the wrong direction. The hourly employees in the plant had recently campaigned to have a union represent them. Emotions ran high during the campaign, but thankfully the company managed to win the election by fifty votes. I was elated, but my boss was upset that the vote had even taken place and suggested that it was a management problem, which was *my* responsibility. I wasn't sure what he meant because I was convinced the problem was not me but those union-pushers in the plant who always wanted something for nothing! The corporate human resources manager even suggested I take a look at my leadership style. That really ticked me off! But she was a liberal, touchy-feely, cause-oriented gal and what did she know about running a large business anyway? She talked theories. I was concerned with results.

Even the Little League baseball team I had volunteered to coach for the last six years was struggling. We won more than our share of games and generally finished respectably in the league, but several parents complained to the head of the league that their kids were simply not having any fun. I knew I could get a little intense and competitive at times—but so what? Two sets of parents even requested that their sons be transferred to other teams. That was a real blow to my ego.

And there was more. I was always a happy-go-lucky, carefree kind of guy with few worries, but now I found myself brooding about practically everything. In spite of all the status and the material toys I possessed, on the inside I was filled with turmoil and conflict. Living for me became a futile exercise of going through the motions. I was becoming moody and withdrawn. Even minor irritations and inconveniences bothered me out of proportion to reality. In fact, it seemed that everyone bugged me. I even annoyed myself.

Of course, I was much too proud to share any of this with others, so I managed to keep everyone fooled. Everyone except Rachael.

OUT OF HER DISTRESS, Rachael firmly suggested that I talk things over with the pastor of our church. In a weak moment I agreed—but my main motivation was to get Rachael off my back. Now understand, I was never the religious type. I always believed church had its place provided it didn't interfere too much with your life.

The pastor suggested I get away by myself for a few days and try to sort things out. He recommended attending a retreat at a small, relatively unknown Christian monastery called John of the Cross, which was located on Lake Michigan near the town of Leeland in the northwestern section of Michigan's Lower Peninsula. The pastor explained that the monastery housed thirty to forty monks of the Order of St. Benedictine, named after the sixth-century monk who devised the "balanced" monastic life. Now, as in the previous fourteen centuries, the monks lived structured lives centered around three priorities—prayer, work, and silence.

Overall, I thought it sounded like a silly idea—something that I would never follow up on—but as I was leaving, the pastor mentioned that one of the monks was a former Fortune 500 executive named Leonard Hoffman.

That caught my attention. I had always wondered what
had ever become of the legendary Len Hoffman.

WHEN I ARRIVED HOME and told Rachael what the
pastor had suggested, she beamed at me. "That's exactly
what I was going to suggest for you, John!" she said. "I
saw a piece on *Oprah* just last week about businessmen
and -women going on spiritual retreats to sort out their
busy lives. You must be meant to go."

Rachael often made comments like that, which irritated me no end. "Meant" to go? What was that supposed to mean?

To make a long story short, I reluctantly agreed to go
to John of the Cross the first week in October—mainly
because I feared Rachael would leave me if I didn't do
something. Rachael drove the six hours to the monastery
and I was silent for most of the trip. My pouting was in-
tended to communicate that I was not happy to be going
to some dreary monastery for an entire week and that
my misery and huge personal sacrifice were for her sake.
Pouting was a tool I had used since I was a kid.

We arrived at the entrance to John of the Cross at
dusk. We turned onto the two-track path and drove up-
hill and back toward the lake about a quarter of a mile.
We parked in a small sandy parking lot next to an old
wooden building with a "Registration" sign nailed to one
of the huge white porch pillars.

A few smaller buildings were scattered around the
premises and all were built on a magnificent sand cliff a

couple of hundred feet above and overlooking Lake Michigan. The setting was beautiful but I didn't mention that to Rachael. After all, I was supposed to be suffering.

"Take care of the kids and house, honey," I said rather coldly as I grabbed my bag out of the trunk, "and I'll call you Wednesday night. Who knows, maybe after this week I'll be the perfect guy you want me to be and then give it all up to become a monk!"

"Very funny, John," she responded while giving me a hug and kiss. With that she was in the car and off in a trail of dust.

I THREW MY BAG over my shoulder and headed toward the registration building. Inside I found a simply furnished, immaculately kept front desk area staffed by a middle-aged man talking on the telephone. He was wearing a black robe that covered him from chin to toe. The gown was gathered at his waist with a length of black rope.

As soon as he hung up the phone, he turned to me and warmly shook my hand. "I'm Father Peter; I help run things here at the guest house. You must be John Daily from downstate."

"That's pretty good, Peter. How did you know who I was?" I replied, not about to address anyone as "Father."

"Just a guess based on the application your pastor sent to us," he answered with a warm smile.

"Who is in charge of things here?" the manager in me wanted to know.

"Brother James has served as our abbot for the past twenty-two years."

"What on earth is an abbot?"

"The abbot is our elected leader and has the final say in all matters concerning our little community. Perhaps you will get a chance to meet him."

"I would like to request a single room this week, Peter, if that's OK with you. I brought some work along with me and I could use some privacy."

"Unfortunately, John, we have only three guest rooms upstairs. Our guests this week include three men and three women, which means that the women will share room number one, our largest room. Our guest from the Army will have room number two to himself, and you will be rooming with Lee Buhr—he's a Baptist minister from Pewaukee, Wisconsin—in room number three. Lee arrived a couple of hours ago and is already settled in. Do you have any other questions?"

"What are the festivities you've got planned for the week?" I asked, somewhat sarcastically.

"In addition to our five daily chapel services, we will have seven days of classroom instruction beginning tomorrow morning and continuing through Saturday morning. Classes will be held in this building from nine to eleven in the morning and again from two to four in the afternoon. In your spare time, you are free to roam the grounds, read, study, talk with our spiritual guides, rest, or do whatever you feel moved to do. The only area that's off limits is the cloistered area where the monks eat and sleep. Is there anything else I can answer for you, John?"

"I'm curious, why do you refer to some of the monks as 'brother' and others as 'father'?"

"Those called 'father' are ordained clergymen while 'brothers' are laypeople from many different walks of life. All of us have made a commitment to work and share our lives together. The thirty-three brothers and fathers share equal stature here. Our names are given to us by the abbot when we take our vows. I arrived here from an orphanage forty years ago, and following my training and vows I was assigned the name Peter."

I finally asked the question I was the most interested in. "I would like to meet Len Hoffman and talk some things over with him. I understand he came here some years ago to join your little group."

"Len Hoffman, Len Hoffman," Peter repeated as he scanned the ceiling, searching his memory. "Oh yes, I think I know who you mean. He also has a different name now. I'm sure he'd love to talk with you. I'll place a note in his mailbox with your request. Come to think of it, he'll be teaching your class on leadership this week. I'm sure you will get a lot out of the class, everyone always does. Good night, sleep well, John, and I hope to see you at the 5:30 chapel service in the morning.

"Oh, and incidentally, John," he continued as I started up the staircase, "Ten years ago the abbot assigned Len Hoffman the name Brother Simeon."

● ● ●

FEELING SOMEWHAT STUNNED, I stopped on the landing at the top of the stairs and stuck my head out the open window to pull in several large breaths of fresh air. It was now nearly pitch black outside and I could hear the waves of Lake Michigan crashing against the shore far below. The wind was howling in from the west at a pretty good clip and the dry autumn leaves were rustling in the huge hardwood trees, sounds I have loved since I was a kid. I could see flashes of lightning on the horizon over the huge, dark lake and I could hear the distant sounds of thunder.

I had an eerie feeling, not uncomfortable or scary, just a sense of déjà vu. "Brother Simeon?" I thought. "This is just a little too weird."

I closed the window and walked slowly down the hallway to look for my room. I quietly opened the door marked with a number three.

A dim orange night light showed me a small yet welcoming room with two twin beds, two desks, and a little couch. A half-open door revealed an attached bathroom. The Baptist preacher was already asleep and softly snoring, curled in the bed by the window.

I suddenly felt very tired. I quickly jumped out of my clothes and into a pair of sweat pants, set my pocket alarm clock for 5:00 A.M., and climbed into bed. As tired as I felt, I didn't honestly believe I would make the 5:30 morning service, but I thought I'd set the alarm as a good faith effort.

I laid my head back on the pillow to sleep, but my mind was spinning crazily. "Find Simeon and listen to him!" Brother Simeon? Had I found him? What kind of a coincidence could this be? How did I ever get myself into this? "You must be *meant* to go"—five church services a day—I can barely handle a couple a month! What am I going to do with myself all week? My dream—what will Simeon be like? What will he have to say to me? Why am I here? "Find Simeon and listen to him!"

The next thing I knew my alarm clock was chirping.

CHAPTER ONE

The Definitions

Being in power is like being a lady.
If you have to remind people that you are,
you aren't. —MARGARET THATCHER

"GOOD MORNING," MY ROOMMATE cheerfully called out to me from his bed before I had even turned my alarm off, "I'm Pastor Lee from Wisconsin. And who might you be?"

"John Daily from downstate. Good to meet you, Lee." I didn't do "Pastor" either.

"We better get dressed if we're going to make it to the 5:30 service."

"You go on ahead. I'm gonna get a little more sack time," I mumbled, trying to sound tired.

"Suit yourself, partner," he quipped and was dressed and out the door in minutes.

I rolled over, pulling the pillow over my head, but soon discovered I was wide awake and feeling a little guilty. Rather than fight it, I quickly washed, dressed, and headed out to find the chapel. It was still dark and the ground was wet from a storm that must have passed over during the night.

I could barely make out the steeple silhouetted against the early morning sky as I made my way over to the chapel. Once inside, I discovered that the old, hexagonal wooden structure was impeccably maintained. The walls were beautifully adorned with stained glass windows, each depicting a different scene. The high, cathedral-style ceiling rose from each of the six walls and converged in the center to form the steeple. There were hundreds of candles burning throughout the sanctuary, the flickering shadows on the walls and stained glass creating an interesting kaleidoscope of shapes and hues. Opposite the door of the church was a simple altar consisting of a small wooden table with the various implements used during the Mass. Immediately in front of the altar and forming a semicircle around it were three rows of eleven simple wooden chairs, obviously set up for the thirty-three monks. Only one of the chairs had arm rests on it. It also had a large crucifix carved into the back support; reserved for the abbot, I assumed. Along one of the walls adjacent to the altar were six folding chairs, which I quickly deduced were for the use of the retreat participants. I quietly made my way over to one of the three vacant chairs and sat down.

My watch said 5:25, yet only half of the thirty-nine chairs were filled. No one spoke as people quietly filed into the chapel, the only sound being the melodic ticking of a huge grandfather clock in the back corner of the chapel. The monks were dressed in their long black robes with rope ties at the waist while the retreat participants were dressed casually. By 5:30, there was a body in every seat.

Suddenly the huge clock in the back began to chime the half hour. The monks immediately rose and began to chant a liturgy, thankfully in English. The retreat participants were given handouts to follow along with but I was quickly lost turning the pages back and forth to the various antiphons, psalms, hymns, and responsive singing sections. I finally gave up trying and just sat back and listened.

I remembered our pastor saying that the monks worshipped in the centuries-old Gregorian format. A year earlier, Rachael had purchased the popular *Chant* CD (a recording of monks in Spain) and I had become very fond of it. This chanting was similar, though the words were in English.

A few of the younger monks referred to their hymnals and other worship guides periodically, but most required no assistance as they moved gracefully through the different parts of the service from memory. Their skills were impressive.

After about twenty minutes or so, the service concluded as suddenly as it had begun and the monks followed the abbot out the back of the church in single file. I glanced at each face as they left, trying to pick out Len Hoffman. Which one was he?

• • •

IMMEDIATELY FOLLOWING the chapel service, I made my way over to the little library, which was just a stone's throw from the chapel. I wanted to do an Internet search and an elderly and extremely helpful monk showed me how to get online.

I found more than one thousand entries on Leonard Hoffman. After over an hour of browsing, I found a decade-old *Fortune* article on Hoffman and read it with fascination.

Len Hoffman graduated from Lake Forest State College in 1941 with a bachelor's degree in business. Soon after, the Japanese attacked Pearl Harbor, taking the life of his best boyhood friend—a devastating blow that led him to join the thousands who were enlisting at that time. Hoffman entered the Navy as a commissioned officer and quickly moved through the ranks before becoming captain of a PT boat assigned to patrol islands in the Philippines. On a routine mission, he was ordered to take prisoner a dozen Japanese, including three officers, who had surrendered after fierce fighting on a small island in his patrol area. Hoffman's directive was to order the Japanese officers and their men to strip naked before proceeding out of the jungle in single file to be handcuffed, loaded on the PT boat, and transported to a destroyer a few miles off the coast. In spite of any animosity he may have held toward the Japanese who had killed his friend at Pearl Harbor, Hoffman did not ask these troops or officers to strip naked and "lose face." He allowed them to emerge from the jungle in full uniform with their arms raised, a dignified officer atop a horse in the lead.

Disobeying the directive of his superior did get him in a little hot water but that quickly passed. Hoffman's only comment about the event was, "It is important to treat other human beings exactly the way you would want them to treat you." Hoffman went on to become a highly decorated officer before his honorable discharge at the end of the war.

As a businessman, the article indicated, Hoffman was very well known and respected as an executive, and his ability to lead and motivate people became legendary in business circles. He became known as a great turnaround artist, taking several companies on the verge of collapse and transforming them into successful going concerns. He was an accomplished author, having written a simple hundred-page book titled *The Great Paradox: To Lead You Must Serve*, which survived in the top fifty on the *New York Times* Best-Sellers List for three years and the top ten on the *USA Today* Money Best-Sellers List for more than five years.

Hoffman's final business accomplishment was to resurrect a former corporate giant, the dying Southeast Air. In spite of annual revenues of over $5 billion, Southeast's poor quality and service and low employee morale made it the laughingstock of the airline industry. Most financial experts believed that Chapter 11 was imminent and Chapter 7 inevitable. The airline had succeeded in losing $1.5 billion in the five years prior to Hoffman's taking over as Chief Executive Officer.

Against these odds, Hoffman led Southeast back to solid financial ground in just over three years. Customer satisfaction and on-time arrivals rose, bringing the airline from the rock bottom of the industry to a solid second place in each measure.

Several of Hoffman's current and former employees, business and military associates, and a few friends had been interviewed for the article. Some spoke freely of their love and affection for him. Some found him to be a deeply spiritual man, though not particularly religious. Others found him to be a man of integrity with highly evolved character traits "not of this world." They *all* spoke of the joy he seemed to have for living. The *Fortune* author even suggested that Len Hoffman appeared to have "figured out the secret to successful living" but did not elaborate further on that point.

The last article I found on the Internet was a follow-up *Fortune* piece from the late 1980s. It seems that when Hoffman was in his mid-sixties and at the peak of his successful career, he resigned his position and dropped out of sight. His wife of forty years had died suddenly from a brain aneurysm the year prior to his resignation, and many believed that this event triggered his departure. The brief article concluded by saying that Hoffman's disappearance was a mystery but rumors had him joining a secret sect or cult of some kind. His five children, all married and with children of their own, provided no information about his whereabouts, only saying that he was happy, healthy, and wished to be left alone.

FOLLOWING THE 7:30 MASS, I was a little chilly and decided to return to my room to put on a sweatshirt before breakfast. When I entered, I heard someone in our tiny bathroom so I yelled, "How's it going, Lee?"

"It's not Lee," came the reply. "I'm just trying to fix this leaky toilet."

I poked my head into the bathroom and found an elderly monk in his black gown on his hands and knees turning a wrench on the toilet pipes. He slowly rose to his feet and I found myself looking up at a man at least three or four inches taller than my six feet. With a rag, he wiped off his hand before extending it to me. "Hello, I'm Brother Simeon. I'm pleased to make your acquaintance, John."

I recognized an older Len Hoffman from the Internet photo with his ruggedly lined face, chiseled cheekbones, prominent chin and nose, and medium-length white hair. He appeared to be in excellent physical condition, with slightly rosy cheeks and a lean, hard body. But what struck me most were his eyes. Clear, deep blue, penetrating eyes. They were the most compassionate and totally accepting set of eyes that I had ever looked into. Simeon also possessed a paradoxical young-old appearance. From his lined face and white hair, one could easily see that he was an elderly man. But his eyes and spirit sparkled and emanated an energy I had only experienced in children.

My hand felt tiny in his huge, powerful hand and I soon found that I was staring at the ground feeling embarrassed. I mean, here was a business legend, someone who was earning well into seven figures a year at the height of his career, fixing my toilet!

"Hi, I'm John Daily . . . it's good to meet you, sir," I weakly offered.

"Oh yes, John. Father Peter mentioned that you wanted to meet with me this—"

"Of course, only if you have the time. I know you must be a very busy man."

He asked with genuine interest, "When would you like to meet, John? Maybe I could suggest—"

"If it's not too much to ask, sir, I would like to spend a little time with you every day that I'm here. Maybe we could eat breakfast together or something. You see, I'm struggling a bit these days and could use some advice. I also have this dream and a few other odd coincidences I would like to tell you about."

I could hardly believe those words were coming out of my mouth! Me—Mr. Got-It-All-Together, Mr. Mask-of-Composure—telling another man I was struggling and needing advice? I was amazed at myself, or was it at Simeon? In less than thirty seconds with this man, my guard was already lowered.

"Let me see what I can do, John. You see, the monks take their meals together in the cloistered section and I would need special permission to join you. Our abbot, Brother James, is usually very reasonable with these types of requests. Until I get permission, how about if we meet at 5 A.M. in the chapel before the first service. That will give us some time to—"

"I would sure appreciate it," I cut him off again, though 5 A.M. sounded pretty rough to me.

"But for now, I need to finish up in here so that I won't be late for breakfast. I'll see you in class at nine sharp."

"See you then, sir," I said, clumsily backing out of the bathroom. I grabbed my sweatshirt and headed down to breakfast, feeling a bit starstruck.

THAT FIRST SUNDAY MORNING, I arrived five minutes early for the instructional session and was pleased to find a medium-size training room, modern and comfortable. Built into two of the walls were beautifully hand-crafted bookshelves, woodwork obviously done by a master of the trade. The west side of the room facing Lake Michigan had a massive stone fireplace, aglow with fragrant white birch wood. The classroom floor was covered with inexpensive but well-kept carpeting that added to the warmth of the room. There were two old but comfortable couches, a La-Z-Boy recliner and a couple of straight-backed wooden chairs (thankfully with pads) arranged in a rough circle, making it impossible to tell where the front of the class might be.

When I arrived, the teacher (Simeon) was standing peering out the window toward the lake, apparently deep in thought. The five other participants were already seated around the circle and I joined my roommate on one of the couches. My watch beeped the hour just as the large clock in the corner chimed nine times. I hastily suppressed the beep as Simeon grabbed a wooden chair and pulled it up to our little group.

"Good morning. I'm Brother Simeon. Over the next seven days, it'll be my privilege to share a few leadership principles that have changed my life. I want you to know that I'm impressed by the collective wisdom present in this room and am eagerly anticipating learning from you. Just think of it. If we were to count up all the years of leadership experience assembled in this circle, how many years do you think we would have? Probably a century or two, wouldn't you think? So we will be learning from one another this week because, please believe me, I do not have all of the answers. But I am a firm believer that all of us together are much wiser than any one of us alone, and together we will make some progress this week. Are you game?"

We all politely nodded our heads, but I was thinking, "Yeah, sure, Len Hoffman could really learn something about leadership from me!"

The teacher asked the six of us to introduce ourselves with a brief bio along with our reasons for attending the retreat.

My roommate—Lee, the preacher—introduced himself first, followed by Greg, a young and rather cocky drill sergeant from the U.S. Army. Theresa, a Hispanic public school principal from downstate spoke next, and then Chris, a tall, attractive, black woman who coached women's basketball at Michigan State University. A woman named Kim introduced herself ahead of me and started telling us about herself but I wasn't listening. I was too busy thinking about what I would say about myself when it was my turn to speak.

As she finished, the teacher looked at me and said, "John, before you begin, I would like to ask you to summarize for us what Kim just said about why she was attending this retreat."

I was shocked by his request and could feel the blood slowly rising up my neck and into my face and head. How was I going to get out of this one? I really had not heard a word of Kim's introduction.

"I'm embarrassed to admit that I didn't hear much of what she said," I stammered, lowering my head. "I apologize to you, Kim."

"Thank you for your honesty, John," the teacher responded. "Listening is one of the most important skills a leader can choose to develop. We'll spend time talking more about that later this week."

"I'll do better," I promised.

After I gave my brief introduction, the teacher said, "I have only one rule this week while we're together. I want you to promise me that if you feel moved to speak that you will speak."

"What does that mean, to be 'moved to speak'?" the sergeant asked skeptically.

"I think you will recognize the feeling when it comes, Greg. It's often an anxious sensation that causes you to begin squirming in your seat, your heart to beat a little faster, or your palms to sweat. It is that feeling when you know you have a contribution to make. Do not deny and attempt to 'stuff' that feeling this week, even when you think the group may not want to hear what you have to say, or you don't feel like saying it. If it *moves* you, speak it. The opposite rule also applies. If you are *not* moved to speak, it is probably better that you refrain from speaking to allow room for others to speak. Trust me now, understand me later. Is that a deal?"

We again politely nodded.

The teacher continued, "All of you are in leadership positions and have people entrusted to your care. I would like to challenge you this week to begin reflecting upon the awesome responsibility you signed up for when you chose to be the leader. That's right, each of you voluntarily signed up to be dad, mom, spouse, boss, coach, teacher, or whatever. Nobody forced you into any of these roles and you are free to leave at any time. In the workplace, for example, employees will spend roughly half their waking hours working and living in the environment you create as the leader. I was amazed when I was in the working world at how nonchalantly and even flippantly people responded to that responsibility. There is a lot at stake and people are counting on you. The role of the leader is a very high calling."

I found myself beginning to feel uncomfortable. I had never really given much thought to how much impact I had on the lives of those I was leading. But a "high calling"? I wasn't so sure.

"The leadership principles I will share with you are neither new nor of my creation. They are as old as the scriptures yet as new and refreshing as this morning's sunrise. These principles apply to each and every leadership role you are privileged to serve in. Please know, if you haven't figured it out already, that it is not by chance you are here in this room today. There is a purpose for your being here and I hope you discover that purpose during our time together this week."

As he spoke I couldn't help but think about the "Simeon coincidences," Rachael's comments, and the series of events that had led me here.

"I have good news and bad news for you today," Simeon continued. "The good news is I will be giving you the keys to leadership over the next seven days. As each of you serves as a leader, I trust this will come as good news to you this morning. Remember that whenever two or more people are gathered together for a purpose there is an opportunity for leadership. The bad news is that each of you must make personal decisions about applying these principles to your lives. Building influence with others, true leadership, is available to everyone but requires a tremendous extension of oneself. Sadly, most of those in leadership positions shy away from the great effort required."

My roommate, the preacher, held his hand up to speak and the teacher nodded at him. "I notice you use the words *leader* and *leadership* a lot and seem to avoid *manager* and *management*. Is that by design?"

"Good observation, Lee. Management is not something you *do* to other people. You manage your inventory, your checkbook, your resources. You can even manage yourself. But you do not manage other human beings. You manage *things*, you *lead* people."

Brother Simeon rose and strolled over to the flip chart, wrote "Leadership" at the top, and asked us to help him define the word. After twenty minutes we came to this definition by consensus:

Leadership: The skill of influencing people to work enthusiastically toward goals identified as being for the common good.

As the teacher returned to his seat he remarked, "One of the key words here is that we have defined leadership as a skill—I have found this to be true. A *skill* is simply a learned or acquired ability. I contend that leadership, influencing others, is a skill set that can be learned and developed by anyone with the appropriate desire coupled with the appropriate actions. The second key word in our definition is *influence*. If leadership is about influencing others, how do we go about developing that influence with people? How do we get people to do our will? How do we get their ideas, commitment, creativity, and excellence, which are by definition voluntary gifts?"

"In other words," I interrupted, "how does the leader get them involved from the 'neck up' rather than just the old 'we only want you from the neck down' mentality. Is that what you mean, Simeon?"

"Precisely, John. To better understand how one develops this type of influence, it is crucial to understand the difference between power and authority. Each and every one of you in this room is in a position of power. But I wonder how many of you have authority with the people you lead."

I was already confused, so I asked, "Simeon, I'm not clear as to the difference between power and authority. Help me out here."

"Glad to, John," Simeon responded. "One of the founders of the field of sociology, Max Weber, wrote a book many years ago called *The Theory of Social and Economic Organization*. In that book, Mr. Weber articulated the differences between power and authority and those definitions are still widely used today. I will para-phrase Mr. Weber as best I can."

The teacher walked back over to the flip chart and wrote:

> *Power:* The ability to force or coerce someone to do your will, even if they would choose not to, be-cause of your position or your might.

"We all know what power looks like, don't we? The world is filled with it. 'Do it or I'll fire you' or 'Do it or we'll bomb you' or 'Do it or I'll beat you up' or 'Do it or I'll ground you for two weeks.' Simply put, 'Do it or else!' Does everyone have their arms around that definition?"

We all nodded affirmatively.

Simeon turned again to the flip chart and wrote:

> *Authority:* The skill of getting people to *willingly* do your will because of your personal influence.

"Now this is something a little bit different isn't it? Authority is about getting people to *willingly* do your will because *you* asked them to do it. 'I'll do it because Bill asked me to do it—I'd walk through walls for Bill' or 'I'll do it because Mom asked me to do it.' And note that power is defined as an *ability* while authority is defined as a *skill*. It doesn't necessarily take any brains or courage to exercise power. Two-year-olds are masters at barking or-ders at their parents and pets. There have been many evil and unwise rulers throughout history. Building authority with people, however, requires a special skill set."

The coach said, "So I am understanding you to say that someone could be in a position of power and not have authority with people. Or conversely, a person could have authority with people but not be in a position of power. Would the goal then be to be a person in power who also has authority with people?"

"That's a splendid way of putting it, Chris! Another way to differentiate between power and authority is to remember that power can be bought and sold, given and taken away. People can be put into positions of power because they're somebody's brother-in-law, somebody's buddy, because they inherited money or power. This is never true with authority. Authority cannot be bought or sold, given or taken away. Authority is about who you are as a person, your character, and the influence you've built with people."

"That may work at home or church but it would never work in the real world!" the sergeant announced.

Simeon almost always addressed people by name. "Let's see if that is really true, Greg. In our homes, for example, would we want our spouse and children to respond to our power or to our authority?"

"Authority, obviously," the principal cut in.

The teacher shot right back, "But why is that so obvious, Theresa? Power would get the job done, wouldn't it? 'Take out the garbage, son, or you're going to get a whipping!' Guess what, the garbage will go out tonight, will it not?"

Kim (who—I'd heard the second time she told me—was the head nurse from the Providence Hospital Birthing Center downstate), chimed in with, "Yes, but for how long? Soon that son is going to grow up and fight back!"

"Exactly, Kim, because power erodes relationships. You can get a few seasons out of power, even accomplish some things, but over time power can be very damaging to relationships. The phenomenon that frequently occurs with teenagers, we call it rebellion, is often a response to being 'powered around' their homes for too long. This same thing happens in business. Employee unrest is often 'rebellion' in disguise."

I suddenly felt nauseous as I thought about my son's behavior and the union drive back at the plant.

"Of course," the teacher continued, "most reasonable people would agree that leading with authority is important in our homes. But what about a volunteer agency? Lee, you're the pastor of a church and you must deal with a lot of volunteers. Is that correct?"

"Indeed I do," the preacher replied.

"Would you say, Lee, that volunteers are more likely to respond to power or to authority?"

Laughing, Lee said, "If we tried to use power with volunteers, they sure wouldn't be around for long!"

"Of course they wouldn't," Simeon continued. "They will only volunteer with an organization that is *meeting their needs.* So how about in the business world. Are we dealing with volunteers in the business world?"

I had to think about that for a minute. My first response was "of course they're not volunteers," but Simeon made me rethink my position.

"Think about it. We can rent their hands, arms, legs, and backs and the market will help us to determine the rent we will pay. But are they not volunteers in even the strictest sense of the word? Are they free to leave? Can they go across the street to another employer for an extra fifty cents an hour? Or even fifty cents less if they really don't like us? Of course they can. And what about their hearts, minds, commitment, creativity, and ideas? Are these not gifts that must be volunteered? Can you order or demand commitment? Excellence? Creativity?"

The coach objected. "Simeon, I think you're living in a dreamland. If you don't exercise power, people will walk all over you!"

"Perhaps, Chris. And lest you think I'm totally a 'pie in the sky' kind of guy, do know that I understand that there are times when we must exercise power. Whether that be in applying the old 'board of education to the seat of learning' in our homes or in firing a bad employee, there are times when we need power. What I am suggesting to you is that when power must be exercised, the leader should reflect on *why* resorting to power was necessary. You see, we had to resort to our power *because* our authority had broken down! Or worse, perhaps we didn't have any authority to begin with."

"But power is the only thing that gets people's attention!" the sergeant insisted.

"That may have been true at one time, Greg," the teacher agreed. "But people respond much differently to power than they used to. Think about what this country has been through during the last thirty years. We've lived through the 1960s and watched the open challenges to power and institutions. We've witnessed abuses of power in our government with Watergate, Irangate, Whitewatergate, You-name-it-gate. We've had some very visible church leaders caught in outrageous and compromising scandals. The military has been caught lying to us with My Lai, Agent Orange, and perhaps now the Gulf War Syndrome. Big business leaders have been openly portrayed by the media and Hollywood as greedy destroyers of the environment—evildoers who cannot be trusted. I believe that many in society today are more skeptical of people in positions of power than ever before."

The preacher interjected, "I was reading in *USA Today* last week that just thirty years ago three out of four people said that they trusted their government. Today that statistic is one out of four. Rather telling, I think."

"This is all fine and good in theory," the coach objected again. "But if, as you say, authority and influence is the way to get things done, then how do you go about building authority with all the different kinds of people we're dealing with today?"

"Patience, Chris, patience," the teacher answered with a chuckle. "We'll be getting to that soon enough."

The sergeant glanced at the clock and called out, "Simeon, I feel moved to speak, so like a good pupil I will speak. Can we adjourn for the morning so that I may go to the can?"

• • •

WE WERE SERVED three substantial meals each day—breakfast at 8:15 A.M. (following morning mass), lunch at 12:30 P.M. (following noon service), and dinner at 6:00 P.M. (following evening vespers). The food was fresh, simply prepared, and delicious, dished up by a pleasant and eager-to-serve monk called Brother Andrew.

Much to my surprise, I managed to attend each of the five daily services during my week at the monastery. Each day began with morning service at 5:30, followed by the mass at 7:30, noon service, evening vespers at 5:30, and compline at 8:30. The services generally lasted from twenty to thirty minutes, each with a slightly varied format depending on the time of day. At first I found the services to be somewhat monotonous but as the week progressed I was surprised to find myself actually looking forward to the next one. The services had a way of centering me and my day and allowed me time to reflect—something I had not done much of in years.

My roommate and I hit it off well together. I found Lee to be a very open person without a lot of pretense, unlike many of the religious types I had met in the past. Although we did not spend much time together, we did share thoughts with one another before retiring at the end of the day. We were usually so tired from the early rising and the daily activities that we would quickly fall asleep anyway. Overall, I couldn't have asked for a better roommate.

As one would expect, the six of us attending the retreat came from different walks of life, our common denominator being that each of us were leaders in our respective organizations. We were all responsible for other people.

The days were structured around the five services, three meals, and four hours of instruction time with short breaks mixed in. We generally spent our remaining time reading, chatting with others, walking the beautiful grounds, or climbing down the 243 stairs to beautiful Lake Michigan for a stroll on the beach.

DURING THE AFTERNOON SESSION, the teacher asked us to pair up with a partner. Kim smiled at me and I joined her, determined to listen this time.

"Let's put some more meat on these bones of building authority, or influence if you prefer, with others. What I would like you to do individually is think of a person in your life, living or dead, who has led you with authority as we defined it earlier today. That could be a teacher, coach, parent, spouse, boss—it doesn't matter. Think of someone who has authority in your life, someone for whom you would walk through walls."

I immediately thought of my dear mother, who had passed away a decade earlier.

"Now with your partner," Simeon continued, "I would like you to list the qualities of character that this person possessed or possesses. Just write them down like a shopping list and then put your two lists together. Then I want the two of you to trim the list down to three to five qualities that would be essential for developing authority with people based on your life experience."

For me this exercise was easy because my mother was a huge influence in my life and I would gladly do more than walk through walls for her, if only I could. I quickly wrote "patient, committed, kind, caring, trustworthy" and passed the sheet to Kim.

I was surprised to discover that Kim's list looked very similar to my own. She had selected a former high school teacher who had made a significant impact in her life.

Simeon went to the flip chart and asked each group for their list. As with Kim, I was amazed at how similar the lists were for each group. The group's top ten answers were:

- Honest, trustworthy
- Good role model
- Caring
- Committed

- Good listener
- Held people accountable
- Treated people with respect
- Gave people encouragement
- Positive, enthusiastic attitude
- Appreciated people

Simeon backed away from the board, remarking, "Great list, great list. We will be coming back to your list later in the week and comparing it with another list that most of you will recognize. But for now, I have two questions about your list. My first question is this. How many of these character qualities that you say are essential for leading with authority are we born with?"

We all spent a minute studying the board before Kim offered a simple, "None of them."

The sergeant objected. "I'm not so sure. A positive, enthusiastic, and appreciative attitude is probably something you're born with. I've never been that kind of guy nor would I especially want to be."

"Oh no? Maybe you could be that kind of guy if I gave you the twenty-five-thousand-dollar challenge," the preacher retorted.

"What do you mean by that, preacherman?" the sergeant shot back.

"Suppose I said I would pay you a twenty-five-thousand-dollar bonus if, over the next six months, you showed a more positive, enthusiastic, and appreciative attitude toward your troops. I have one question for you,

Greg. Would I or would I not witness some major 'sucking up' coming out of you toward your troops?"

Amid snickers the sergeant lowered his nodding head saying, "I see your point, preacher."

Simeon rescued Greg with, "All of these traits you've listed are behaviors. And behavior is a choice. My second question is, How many of these ten traits, behaviors, do you currently display in your lives?"

"All of them," the principal answered. "To some degree we do all of them. Some better than others and some perhaps very poorly. I could be the worst listener in the world, but I am still forced to listen on occasion. I could be a very dishonest person yet still be honest in dealing with my family."

"Wonderful, Theresa," the teacher said with a smile. "These traits are often developed early in life and become habitual ways of behaving. Some of our habits, our character traits, continue to evolve and mature to higher levels, while others change little from adolescence. The challenge for the leader is to pick the character traits that need work and apply Lee's twenty-five-thousand-dollar challenge to them. Challenge ourselves to change our habits, change our character, change our nature. *That* requires a choice and a lot of effort."

"A person can't change his nature," the sergeant said defiantly.

"Stay tuned, Greg, there's more to come," the teacher replied with a twinkle in his eye.

• • •

FOLLOWING THE MIDAFTERNOON BREAK, we spent the remainder of the day discussing the importance of relationships.

The teacher began, "Simply put, leadership is about getting things done through people. When working with and getting things done through people, there will always be two dynamics involved—the task and the relationship. It is easy for leaders to lose their balance by focusing on only one of these dynamics at the expense of the other. For example, if we focus only on getting the task done and not on the relationship, what symptoms may arise?"

"Oh that's easy," the nurse responded. "You can tell the taskmasters at our hospital by watching who has the greatest turnover in their departments. Nobody wants to work for them."

"Exactly, Kim. If we focus only on tasks and not on the relationship, we may experience turnover, rebellion, poor quality, low commitment, low trust, and other undesirable symptoms."

"Yeah," I offered much to my surprise. "I recently went through a union drive back where I work because we were probably too focused on the task. All I preached was the bottom line and the relationship probably suffered."

"But the task is important!" the sergeant pointed out. "None of us will be working for long if the job's not getting done."

"You are absolutely correct, Greg," Simeon agreed. "If the leader is not accomplishing the tasks at hand but is only concerned with the relationship, that may be good baby-sitting but certainly not effective leadership. The key then to leadership is *accomplishing the tasks at hand while building relationships*."

I had a thought I felt moved to share. "I think this may be changing a little, but many if not most of the people promoted into leadership positions these days are promoted because of their technical or task-related abilities. It's a common pitfall that I've been warned against many times in my career. We promote our best fork lift driver to supervisor and now we've created two new problems. We've got a lousy supervisor and we've lost our best fork lift driver! So because of this flawed tendency, task or technically oriented people are probably in the majority of leadership positions."

"That may well be true, John," the teacher replied. "Earlier we said that power can be very hard on relationships. Now we need to ask the next question. Are relationships important where you lead? It took me nearly a lifetime to learn the great truth that *all* of life is relational—with God, self, and others. And this is even and perhaps especially true in business because without people there is no business. Healthy families, healthy teams, healthy churches, healthy businesses, and even healthy lives are about healthy relationships. The truly great leaders are skilled at building healthy relationships."

41

"Could you be more specific, Simeon?" the coach challenged. "I usually think of business as being about brick, mortar, and machines. Just what relationships are you talking about?"

"To have a healthy and thriving business, there must be healthy relationships with the C.E.O.S. in the organization and I am *not* referring to the Chief Executive Officers. I am talking about the *Customers*, the *Employees*, the *Owners* (or Stockholders), and the *Suppliers*. For example, if our customers are leaving and going to the competition, we have a relationship problem. We are not identifying and meeting their legitimate needs. And rule number one in business is that if we do not meet the needs of our customers, someone else will."

That got a reaction from me, "Yeah, the old days of wining and dining the customer and getting the order are over. Now it's about quality, service, and pricing."

The teacher agreed. "That's right, John, meeting the customer's legitimate *needs*. The same principle is true with employees. Labor unrest, turnover, strikes, low morale, low trust, and low commitment are merely symptoms of a relationship problem. The legitimate needs of the employees are not being met."

I immediately recalled my boss telling me that the union campaign at the plant was a management problem and I had chosen not to listen to him.

"Let me take this a step further. If we are not meeting the needs of the owners or stockholders, the organization will also be in serious trouble. The stockholders have a legitimate need to get a fair return on their investment—and if we are not meeting that need as an organization, then our relationship with the stockholders will not be very good."

The preacher offered, "That's right, Brother Simeon. And if the stockholders aren't happy, we aren't going to be around for long as an organization. I found that out in a very painful way many years ago when I was G.M. of a large resort in Arizona. We were all having a lot of fun at work and not mindful of the bottom line, until the wake-up call came. I went from the unemployment line directly into the seminary."

The teacher marched on. "The same relationship principle is true with our vendors and suppliers, whether it be parts, services, or funding to operate our organizations. A healthy symbiotic relationship between supplier and customer is necessary for the long-term health of any organization. In summary then, healthy relationships with the customers, employees, owners, and suppliers (the C.E.O.S.) ensure healthy business. Effective leaders understand this simple principle."

The sergeant wasn't convinced. "But in the end, Simeon, do you know what is really going to make and keep the troops, employees, or whoever happy? The answer is always 'Show me the money!' "

"Money, of course, is important, Greg. Just withhold a paycheck and you'll quickly discover how important it is. However, for decades surveys done in this country on what people want most from their organizations have consistently shown money down at number four or five on the list. Being treated with dignity and respect, being able to contribute to the success of the organization, feeling in on things, always rank higher than money. Unfortunately, most leaders have made the choice not to believe the surveys."

The preacher, who was squirming in his chair and quite obviously moved to speak, finally said, "Think of the institution of marriage in this country—roughly half of these partnerships, you could call them organizations, fail. Do you know the number one reason given for the failure? Money and financial problems! Now how many of you believe that? That's like saying that poor people cannot have good marriages! How absurd! Having counseled couples for years in my pastoral role, I can assure you that money is what everyone points to when there are problems because it is tangible and we can grasp it. But a poor relationship is always at the root of things."

"Good point," I jumped in. "During a recent union drive at our plant, everyone kept telling me that the main issue was money until I became convinced that it was. But the union-buster consultant we hired to help us get through the union campaign kept telling me that the issue was *not* money. He insisted it was a relationship problem but I didn't believe him. Perhaps he was right."

The principal asked, "Simeon, if relationships are so important in organizations and in life, and I happen to agree with you, then what do you believe is the most important ingredient in a successful relationship?"

"Glad you asked, Theresa," the teacher quickly replied. "And the answer is simple: trust. Without trust, it is difficult if not impossible to maintain a good relationship. Trust is the glue that holds relationships together. If you aren't quite sure about this principle, then ask yourself this question: How many good relationships do you have with people you do not trust? Are you eager to have dinner with those people on Saturday night? Without basic levels of trust, marriages break up, families dissolve, organizations topple, countries collapse. And trust comes from being trustworthy. More about that later in the week."

I am sure that we discussed much more in that first lesson on that first Sunday in October, but these are the main points I recall. I had so many thoughts and emotions going on at once that I had great difficulty paying attention toward the end of the day. I kept thinking about the responsibilities that I had "signed up" for: boss, dad, husband, coach—and those responsibilities juxtaposed with my power style of leadership gave me a sinking feeling. I was feeling depressed and thoroughly exhausted as I collapsed into bed that night.

CHAPTER TWO

The Old Paradigm

If you do not change your direction,
you will end up exactly where you are headed.
—ANCIENT CHINESE PROVERB

I WAS WIDE AWAKE at 4:45 A.M. but didn't feel much like getting out of bed. I knew the teacher would be waiting for me at the chapel so I dragged myself out from under the warm covers, threw some water on my face, and made my way over to find him.

Simeon was sitting in the same chair he occupied for the five daily services. He waved me over and I sat down next to him.

"Sorry to get you out of bed to meet me this early," I apologized.

"Oh not at all, I've been up for some time now, John. I'm glad to be able to spend some time with you. I asked the abbot yesterday about meeting for breakfast with you but he has yet to give me an answer. He did agree to allow us to break the Great Silence before 5:30 service and I'm grateful for that."

"That's really big of him," I thought to myself.

"So tell me, John, what have you been learning?"

"All kinds of things," I nonchalantly replied. "That whole power and authority thing was interesting. But hey, Simeon, you really got me on not listening to Kim yesterday."

"Oh yes, John. I have noticed that you don't listen very well."

"What do you mean?" I asked defensively. "I've always thought of myself as a pretty good listener."

"Yesterday morning when we met in your room, you cut me off in midsentence no less than three times. Now my ego can handle that, John, but I'm afraid of the messages you send to the people you are leading when you cut them off like that. Haven't others told you of this bad habit you've developed?"

"No, not really," I lied, knowing that one of Rachael's biggest complaints with me was that I never let people finish a sentence before throwing in my two cents. It frustrated my kids to no end. Rachael always maintained that I probably did the same thing at work and insisted that nobody would ever have the courage to tell me to my face. Yet one time at work somebody did just that. It was during an exit interview with a production manager who was resigning to go work for the competition. He told me that I was the worst listener he had ever met. I didn't pay much attention at the time because I figured that quitters and traitors didn't know much anyway.

"When you cut people off in midsentence like that, John, it sends some bad messages. Number one, by cutting me off you obviously have not been listening to me very well if you've already formulated your response in your head; two, you do not value me or my opinion because you refuse to take the time to hear me out; and finally, you must believe that what you've got to say is much more important than what I've got to say. John, these are disrespectful messages you just can't afford to send as the leader."

"But that's not the way I feel, Simeon," I objected. "I have a great deal of respect for you."

"Your *feelings* of respect must be aligned with your *actions* of respect, John."

"I guess I'll have to work on that," I replied hurriedly, wanting to change the subject.

"Tell me about yourself, John," the teacher asked as if reading my mind.

I gave Simeon a five-minute autobiography and another five-minute description of the "Simeon coincidences" and my recurring dream.

Simeon listened intently as if nothing else in the world mattered but what I was saying. He looked directly into my eyes, nodded his head periodically to acknowledge that he understood, but he never spoke a word until I was completely finished.

After a minute or two of silence, he said, "Thank you for sharing your story, John. That was fascinating. I love to hear about people's journeys through life."

"Oh, nothing so special," I said in a discounting way. "So tell me, what do you think about all these Simeon coincidences?"

"I'm not sure yet, John," he said, rubbing his chin. "I tend to agree with your wife that there is probably something to them. Our unconscious mind and the dreams it gives us has untold riches that we are only beginning to understand."

"Yeah, I suppose."

"So how can I be of assistance to you this week, John?"

"I guess I would just like to pick your brain some if I could, Simeon. I really am struggling a bit these days and my mind is restless. You would think a guy who has everything anyone could ask for would be content and happy. But as I just told you, that's not the case with me."

"John, it took me many years to learn that it is not the material things in life that will bring you joy," he said as if stating a universal truth. "Just look around us. The greatest pleasures in life are absolutely free."

"Do you really think so, Simeon?"

"Just for openers, John, think about love; marriage; families; friends; children; grandchildren; sunsets; sunrises; moonlit nights; twinkling stars; little babies; the gifts of touch, taste, smell, hearing, eyesight; good health; flowers; lakes; clouds; sex; the ability to make choices; and even life itself. They are all free, John."

A few monks were beginning to file into the chapel and I knew our time was nearly up.

"I guess I'm supposed to learn something from you this week, Simeon. I don't know what that could be but I'm willing to play along. I do know that I've got to get my life back together again before I lose my job or even my family. But to be honest with you, I'm actually feeling worse here, not better. The more I listen to you the more off track I realize I've been. I don't think I have ever felt this low."

"That is the perfect place to begin," Simeon replied.

THE CLASSROOM WAS BUZZING when the clock began its nine chimes that Monday morning.

The teacher smiled around the group and said gently, "I suspect a few of you have been struggling with some of the principles we discussed yesterday."

"You're damn right we are!" the sergeant exploded, as if speaking for the whole group. "This fairyland talk goes against everything we've learned out there in the real world."

The preacher shook his head and said, "What do you mean, 'we'? Maybe you're just going to have to challenge some of your old paradigms, soldier!"

"And what's a paradigm, preacher?" the sergeant growled back. "Something you got out of your Bible?"

Simeon took over. "Paradigm, now that's a good word. Paradigms are simply psychological patterns, models, or maps we use to navigate our way through life. Our paradigms can be helpful and even life saving when used appropriately. They can, however, become dangerous if we assume our paradigms are never-changing and all-encompassing truths and allow them to filter out the new information and the changing times that are coming at us throughout life. Clinging to outdated paradigms can cause us to become stuck while the world passes us by."

The sergeant said, "OK, now I get it. My old paradigm was that monks were weird and that monasteries were to be avoided at all costs! Thanks to my captain, who insisted on sending me here, I'm pleased to say that those paradigms are being challenged here this week!" He rolled his eyes.

We all laughed, and no one laughed harder than Simeon.

"Thanks, Greg, I think," the teacher responded with a smile. "As an example of a dangerous paradigm, think about the worldview a little girl with an abusive father might develop. The idea—the paradigm—that grown men are not to be trusted would serve her well as a child, leading her to stay out of her father's way. However, if she transfers that paradigm into the adult world as she grows older, she will probably run into severe difficulties with men."

"I understand," the nurse remarked. "The little girl's paradigm was that all men are not to be trusted but the appropriate paradigm is that *some* men are not to be trusted. So a model that served her well while living at home with that jerk was inappropriately transferred into a different and larger context in the adult world."

"Exactly, Kim," Simeon continued. "It is therefore important that we continually challenge our paradigms about ourselves, the world around us, our organizations, and other people. Remember, the outside world enters our consciousness through the filters of our paradigms. And our paradigms are not always accurate."

I added, "I read somewhere that we do not see the world as it is—we see the world as *we* are. The world looks very different depending on your perspective. The world looks different if I am rich or poor, sick or healthy, young or old, or black or white. . . . My wife sees the world much differently than I do, believe me."

The principal offered, "I believe it was Mark Twain who said that we must be careful to glean the appropriate lesson from our experiences lest we be like the cat who sits on a hot stove. Because the cat who sits on a hot stove will never again sit on a *hot* stove but she will never sit on a *cold* one either."

"Excellent, excellent," the teacher responded with his usual smile. "Think of the old paradigms. The world is flat, the sun revolves around the earth, salvation comes by being a good person, women should not vote, black people are inferior, monarchies should rule the people, white spiked shoes should not be worn on the football field, long hair and earrings are for women only—you get the idea. New ideas and ways of doing things will often be challenged, even labeled as heretical, works of the devil, communistic. Challenging the old ways takes a lot of effort but so does the alternative. The world is changing so quickly that we can become stuck—or worse—if we don't challenge our beliefs and paradigms."

The coach stated, "I wonder if that is why continuous improvement is so big these days. If an organization is not challenging its beliefs and old ways of doing things, the competition and the world just passes it by. But change is so hard for people. Why do you think that is, Simeon?"

The teacher responded quickly. "Change takes us out of our comfort zone and forces us to do things differently, and that's hard. Challenges to our ideas force us to rethink our position, and that's always uncomfortable. Rather than working through things and tolerating hard work and discomfort, many are content to stay forever stuck in their little ruts."

"A rut," the principal asserted with a grin, "is little more than a coffin with the ends kicked out."

The coach volunteered, "Continuous improvement is crucial for people as well as organizations because nothing stays the same in life. Nature shows us clearly that you are either alive and growing or you are dying, dead, or decaying."

The teacher added, "Almost everyone buys into the idea of continuous improvement but by definition it is impossible to *improve* unless we *change*. It's those brave souls on the cutting edge who are challenging and asking the questions that will lead the way for others."

"George Bernard Shaw," the principal chimed in again, "once said that the reasonable man adapts himself to the world; the unreasonable one persists in trying to adapt the world to himself; therefore, all progress depends on the unreasonable man."

"I often tell my players," added the coach, "that it is best to be the lead dog on a dog sled for three reasons. One, you get to cut the fresh snow, two, you are first to see the new scenery, and three, you're not looking up at a bunch of rear-ends all the time!"

"Thanks, Chris, I hadn't heard that one," the teacher chuckled.

He walked over to the flip chart and wrote down examples of old and new paradigms as the group brainstormed together.

OLD PARADIGM	NEW PARADIGM
U.S. invincibility	Global competition
Centralized management	Decentralized management
Japan = junk products	Japan = quality products
Management	Leadership
I think	Cause and effect
If it ain't broke . . .	Continuous improvement
Short-term profit	Balance short- and long-term profit
Labor	Associates
Avoid and fear change	Change is a constant
It's good enough	Zero defects

Simeon continued, "Of course, we have old paradigms about running organizations that may need to be challenged as we enter the new millennium. Like the little girl, we may be carrying old baggage and inappropriate organizational paradigms into a new and ever-changing world. What would you say are the predominant paradigms about running an organization today?"

The sergeant, as usual, was quick to jump on that one. "Pyramid style of management. Top down. Do as I say. If I want your opinion I'll give it to you. Living by the golden rule that says 'He who has the gold makes the rules.'"

"I think you've pretty much nailed it, Greg," the principal chimed in. "And it doesn't really seem to be changing. Our new generation of leaders, the Baby Boomers and Generation Xers—well, for a while some of us hoped they might do it differently and perhaps better, but they seem to be following in the footsteps of their predecessors."

Simeon slowly walked over to the flip chart again, saying, "Let's talk about the pyramid style of management paradigm and how it came to be so popular in our country."

He drew a large triangle and subdivided it into five sections. "Our top-down pyramid style of management is a very old concept borrowed from centuries of war and monarchies. In the military, for example, we have the general at the top, with colonels or whoever on the next level, followed by captains and lieutenants beneath them, then the sergeants, and guess who gets to be on the bottom?"

"The grunts!" said Greg. "The front line troops often refer to themselves as the grunts and they're damned proud of it too!"

"Thank you, Greg. And who is the one in closest contact with the enemy?" Simeon continued. "The general or Greg's grunts?"

"Well, of course the grunts are," the coach replied.

The teacher began to fill in typical organizational titles above the military titles, saying, "Let's go one step further and translate this military model into our organizations today. Let's put the CEO in the general's slot, the vice presidents with the colonels, the middle managers with the captains and lieutenants, and the supervisors with the sergeants. Now guess who gets to be on the bottom in the typical organization?"

"The grunts," three of us answered in unison.

"Not anymore," the preacher announced. "We have now become enlightened and refer to them as the associates!"

"Thank you, Lee," the teacher smiled. "And where is the customer in this model? Who is closer to the customer, the CEO or the folks doing the work and adding value to the product? I hope the answer is obvious to you."

I offered, "My business mentor used to remind me that the people putting the glass in the boxes out on our factory floor are the ones closest to the customer. I mean, I may personally know the customers and may even take them to lunch occasionally, but the most

OLD PARADIGM

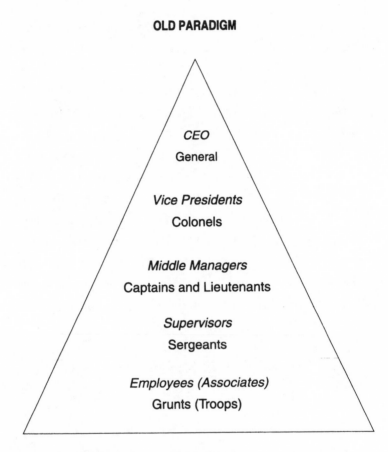

CEO
General

Vice Presidents
Colonels

Middle Managers
Captains and Lieutenants

Supervisors
Sergeants

Employees (Associates)
Grunts (Troops)

Customer
Enemy

important thing to the customers is what is inside that box when they remove the cover. And the last person to touch that glass is the worker on the floor. I guess that makes them closer to the customer."

"Yeah, I've heard executives say that it's lonely at the top. But they're all alone because everyone else is out getting the job done!" Theresa blurted out.

"And so you get a model that looks something like this," Simeon announced, backing away from the flip chart.

"Is this a good model or paradigm for running an organization today?" the teacher asked.

"One thing's for sure, it is an effective way to get things done!" the sergeant replied somewhat defensively. "The old U S of A has kicked some major butt using this style—it's been successful for a long time."

"Well," the preacher commented, "it does only seem natural after the great victories this country had earlier in the century that people would return home believing this top-down, obey-orders-without-question, power style of running things would be *the* way to get things done. Many people probably returned home thinking that this was the best, and perhaps the only, way to run their businesses, homes, sports teams, churches, and other nonmilitary organizations."

"No question that the military model was effective in winning wars," the teacher agreed, nodding. "I am free and thankful for that freedom as I stand here today. But I wonder, like the little abused girl I spoke of earlier, if we have inappropriately transferred a perfectly good model when defending homelands and babies into a world where the model will not be as effective. Does this model serve us well today or is there a better way?"

"You know," Lee began, "as I look at the model on your flip chart, I am struck that we have the customer in the same place as the enemy. You don't really believe that organizations view the customer as the enemy, do you?"

"I would certainly hope not, at least not consciously," Kim replied. "But, as I look at this top-down style of management, I am concerned about the messages that are being sent to the organization."

"What do you mean by that?" I queried.

"Everyone in the organization is looking upward, toward the boss and away from the customer," came her quick reply.

"Beautiful observation, Kim!" Simeon exclaimed. "And that is exactly what happens with a top-down mentality or paradigm. If I were to go into your organizations and ask your employees—associates or whatever you call them—Who are you trying to please, or Who is it that you serve, what do you think the response of the vast majority of the people would be?"

I jumped on that one. "I'd like to think they would say 'the customer' but I'm afraid they would say 'the boss.' Yes, in fact I'm quite sure that the employees in my plant would say something like, 'I'm here to make sure the boss is happy. As long as the boss is happy, life is good.' Sad, but most likely true."

"That's honest, John," the teacher acknowledged. "My experience has been the same. The people in many organizations today are looking up the food chain, so to speak, and worrying about keeping the boss happy. And while everyone is focusing on keeping the boss happy, who's focusing on keeping the customer happy?"

The principal looked a bit troubled as she slowly said, "How ironic and sad. Maybe the pyramid is upside down. Maybe the customer needs to be at the top. Doesn't that make more sense?"

"It sure does make sense, Theresa," the preacher replied, "because if the customer is not being served and kept happy, we're not going to have much to talk about at the next seminar because we'll soon be out of business."

The teacher walked over to the flip chart, saying, "Following through with what Theresa said, suppose that our top-down paradigm is upside down. Suppose a perfectly good model for one place and time is not appropriate for today. What if, as Theresa suggested, we invert the triangle and place the customer at the top. And as we said earlier, the closest one to the customer would be the associates or employees, supported by the front-line supervisor, and then all the rest. The new model might look something like this."

Simeon backed away from the flip chart.

"I think you're living in la-la land, Simeon," the sergeant insisted. "You're saying the employees would be at the top running the place. I mean, all this warm and fuzzy talk is fun in theory—but forget it in the real world."

NEW PARADIGM

Customer

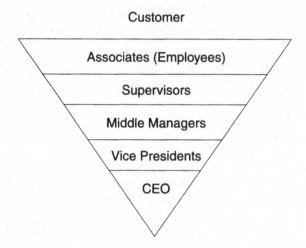

Associates (Employees)

Supervisors

Middle Managers

Vice Presidents

CEO

"Please bear with me here for another minute or two, Greg," Simeon said. "Let's just imagine an organization where the focus was serving the customer on top. Imagine, as the upside-down pyramid depicts, an organization where the front-line employees are truly serving the customers and ensuring that their legitimate needs are being met. And just suppose the front-line supervisors began seeing their employees as their customers and set about the task of identifying and meeting their needs. And so on down the pyramid. That would require each manager to take on a new mind-set, a new paradigm, and recognize that the role of the leader is not to rule and lord it over the next layer down. Rather, the role of the leader is to serve. What an interesting paradox. What if we had it upside down all along? Perhaps we lead best by serving."

The nurse interjected, "I always tell my department supervisors that their job is to remove all the obstacles, all the roadblocks in their people's way in getting the patients served. I tell them to picture themselves as giant pavement levelers removing all the speed bumps along the way for their people. I guess to put it in your words, Simeon, removing the obstacles would be serving the people."

"That's right," the preacher added. "Unfortunately, too many managers spend their careers getting *in the way* instead of getting the obstacles *out of the way*. In my previous life we used to call supervisors who spent their days getting in the way 'seagull managers.' A seagull manager is one who periodically flies into the area, makes a lot of noise, dumps on people, maybe eats their lunch, and flies away. I think we've all known a few managers like that in our time."

"My boss takes it a step further," the nurse added again. "She tells me that management is all overhead. She says that when we as managers stopped serving coffee on the airplanes, cleaning out the bedpans, teaching the kids in school, or driving the fork lift, we have ceased adding value to the product or service and have become overhead."

"I'm not sure if it's worse to be called 'overhead' or a 'seagull manager,'" the teacher responded, chuckling. "It is a shame that so many leaders spend their time pondering their *rights* as leaders instead of their awesome *responsibilities* as leaders."

"Even in negotiating a union contract," I said slowly, "the company and the union often spend countless hours fighting over the 'Management Rights' section of the contract. I once heard of a union official at one of our sister companies who yelled back over the conference table, 'How about if I give you some lefts to go along with them rights!'"

"It's time for noon chapel," Simeon said, smiling. "In summary then, a leader is someone who identifies and meets the legitimate needs of their people, removes all the barriers, so they can serve the customer. Again, to lead you must serve."

"Earth to Simeon, earth to Simeon!" the sergeant chanted under his breath on the way out the door.

AFTER LUNCH, I decided to go for a brief stroll along the beach before the afternoon session. Greg asked if he could join me and I lied politely, "That would be great." The sergeant was about the last person on earth that I wanted to go for a stroll with.

We walked a couple of minutes in silence before he asked, "What do you think of all this power versus authority and serving the people stuff?"

"Not sure yet, but I'm still listening," I replied.

"I have a hard time believing that it could really work this way in the real world. It's Greek to me."

"You and me both, Greg," I said, just to be agreeable.

But for the second time in less than five minutes I was lying to Greg. The teacher's words were not some foreign language to me. I recognized *truth* when I heard it.

ALL WERE PRESENT and curiously quiet when the clock chimed twice to begin our afternoon session.

Simeon didn't get the first word out when the sergeant spoke up. "I know you were supposed to be a good leader years ago and I respect that, Simeon. But I can't believe you accomplished what you did by telling supervisors to do whatever the employees want! If I tried to manage, excuse me, lead people that way, I would have open anarchy. In a perfect world you may be right, but doing what people want will never work in this world, big guy."

"I'm sorry, Greg," the teacher began, "I guess I have not made it very clear about what it means to be the servant. I said that leaders should identify and meet the *needs* of their people, *serve* them. I did not say that they should identify and meet the *wants* of their people, be *slaves* to them. Slaves do what others *want*, servants do what others *need*. There is a world of difference between meeting wants and meeting needs."

"And how would you define the difference?" Greg asked, a bit more calmly.

Simeon didn't miss a beat. "As a parent, for example, if I were to allow my children to do whatever they want, how many of you would want to spend time at my home? Not too many of you, I suspect, because the kids would be running the place, we'd have 'anarchy,' as you put it. By giving in to what they want, I am certainly not giving them what they need. Children and adults need an environment with boundaries, a place where standards are set and people are held accountable. They may not *want* boundaries and accountability but they *need* boundaries and accountability. We don't do anybody any favors by running undisciplined homes or departments. The leader should never settle for mediocrity or second best—people have a need to be pushed to be the best they can be. It may not be what they want, but the leader should always be more concerned with needs than with wants."

To my surprise I felt moved to speak so I added, "The employees working in our plant all want to make twenty dollars an hour. Now if we were to pay them twenty dollars an hour we would probably be out of business in a matter of a few months because our competition could make the glass much cheaper. So in the end, we may have done what the employees *wanted*, but we sure didn't do what the employees *needed*, which is providing stable, long-term employment."

The sergeant added, "Yeah, think about how politicians make their policy decisions based on the most recent Gallup poll. I guess they're giving people what they want, but I wonder if it's what they need."

"But how do you clearly differentiate between needs and wants?" the nurse asked.

"A want," the teacher explained, "is simply a wish or desire without any regard for the physical or psychological consequences. A need, on the other hand, is a legitimate physical or psychological requirement for the well-being of a human being."

"Doesn't that get a bit tricky?" Kim questioned. "After all, people are different and so it follows naturally that they would have different needs. Although I suspect that there are certain needs, like being treated with respect, that are universal."

"Great point, Kim," I jumped in. "My oldest, John Jr., was a strong-willed child while my daughter, Sarah, was the compliant one. They certainly have different needs and it has required different parenting styles to handle those individual needs. The same is true where I work. A new employee certainly has a different set of needs than a twenty-year employee who knows his or her job better than I could ever dream of knowing it. Different people do have different needs, so I guess the leader needs to be flexible."

The teacher pressed on. "If the role of the leader is to identify and meet the legitimate needs of the people, then we should be constantly asking ourselves, What are the needs of the people I lead? I would challenge you to make a list of the needs your people have, in your home, in church, in school, wherever you lead. And if you get stuck on what the people need, then just ask yourself, What needs do *I* have? That should get you going again."

Greg said, "Well, Chucky driving the fork lift at work needs a good-running machine, proper tools, training, materials, fair pay, and a safe work environment. That should make him happy."

Simeon replied, "That's a very good start, Greg—it pretty well covers his physical needs. But remember, Chucky also has psychological needs that must be met. What might those needs be?"

The nurse—the brightest of the retreat participants, I thought—rose and walked over to the flip chart and drew yet another pyramid.

She began, "I can't believe I'm doing this but I'll do what Simeon asked, which is to speak when I feel moved to speak."

"Teacher's pet!" I yelled at Kim.

"Stop it, John! This is hard for me," she shot back with a little smile. "Psych 101 in college taught us about Abraham Maslow and his hierarchy of human needs. I think there were five levels of needs with the lowest level being food, water, and shelter, the second tier being safety and security needs, and so on."

The nurse backed away from the flip chart before resuming. "As I recall, the lower-level needs must first be met before the higher-level needs become motivators. So on the lowest tier, I suppose paying a fair wage and benefit would sufficiently meet the food, water, and shelter needs. The second-tier needs would include safety and security needs, which at work could mean a safe work environment along with providing boundaries and

MASLOW'S HIERARCHY OF HUMAN NEEDS

setting the standards as Simeon said earlier. This in turn provides consistency and predictability—which, as I recall Maslow saying, was crucial to meeting safety and security needs. Maslow was not at all a supporter of permissive parenting."

"Go on, Kim!" Theresa encouraged. "You're really on a roll!"

Kim broke into a big grin as she continued, her nervousness fading. "Anyway, once those needs are met, the belonging and love needs become motivators. As I recall, that includes the need to be a part of a healthy group with accepting and healthy relationships. Once *those* needs are met, the motivator becomes self-esteem, which includes the need to be valued, treated with respect, appreciated, encouraged, to receive recognition, rewards, and so on."

"Yeah, make sure you get in the warm and fuzzy stuff," the sergeant teased.

"Moving right along," the nurse continued, smiling. "Once these needs are met, the need moves to self-actualization, which many have struggled trying to define. What I got out of it was that to self-actualize is to become the best you can be or are capable of becoming. Not everyone can be president of the company, All-American, or valedictorian. But everyone can be the best employee, player, or student possible. And if I'm understanding Simeon correctly, the leader should push and encourage people to become the best they are capable of becoming. I guess Chucky on the fork lift may never be president of the company, but we can encourage and push him to be the best fork lift driver he can be."

"Be all that you can be, now that sounds familiar, doesn't it, Greggy boy?" the preacher snickered. "Isn't that the Army theme song in those commercials that drive us all nuts? I think we should all sing it for Greg."

As we adjourned for the day, we marched out the door singing the Army jingle at the top of our lungs.

CHAPTER THREE

The Model

*Anyone wanting to be the leader must
first be the servant. If you want to lead
you must serve.* —JESUS CHRIST

THE TEACHER WAS SITTING and waiting when I arrived at the chapel a few minutes after five Tuesday morning.

"Good morning, John," he cheerfully greeted me.

"Sorry I'm late," I responded, still a little groggy. "You look bright and chipper. What time do you usually get up in the morning?"

"Quarter to four, except for Sunday mornings. That gives me some time to get centered before the first service."

"That's too early for me," I said, shaking my head.

"So tell me, John, what have you been learning?"

"I don't know, Simeon. I find myself getting really irritated with Greg and it's hard for me to concentrate. It seems like he challenges everything. I guess it must be his Army training or something. Why don't you put him in his place or just ask him to leave instead of letting him disrupt everything?"

"I pray for people just like Greg to be in my classes."

"You actually *want* guys like that in your class?" I asked incredulously.

"You bet I do. My first mentor in business taught me a hard lesson about the importance of contrary opinion. As a young vice president at a sheet metal manufacturing company, I tended to be an extreme Theory Y, let's-hold-hands-and-have-fun kind of leader. A couple of other vice presidents, who I remember vividly to this day, Jay and Kenny, were two extreme Theory X types who believed that people were lazy, dishonest, and needed to be prodded with sticks to get them to work."

"Kind of like Greg?"

"I have no idea what Greg believes, John, but I do know that things are not always as they appear. We should be careful before making quick judgments. In addition, Greg is not here to defend himself, and I try very hard not to talk negatively about those who are not present."

"Probably a good personal policy to have," I nodded.

"I've tried to live, many times unsuccessfully, with the philosophy that we should never treat people differently from the way we would want to be treated. I don't think we would want people talking about us behind our backs, would we, John?"

"Good point, Simeon."

"Back to Jay and Kenny. I would go into our executive meetings with the other VPs and have tremendous conflict whenever employee issues were discussed. Those two guys were always pushing for tougher policies and procedures and I was always pushing for a more democratic and open style of management. I always believed Jay and Kenny would ruin the company with their 'way of the dinosaur' attitudes. At the same time Jay and Kenny always believed that I was a closet pinko-commie who wanted to give away the company. My boss, Bill—the president of the company and a personal friend—would patiently referee these battles, some of them fierce, sometimes siding with them, sometimes with me."

"Tough spot for him to be in," I suggested.

"Not for Bill," he quickly replied. "Bill always had clear boundaries, and especially when it came to the needs of the business. After a particularly heated meeting one day, I pulled Bill aside and said, 'Why don't you just fire those two idiots so that we can start having some civil and upbeat meetings?' I will remember his response to my dying day."

"He agreed to fire them?"

"On the contrary, John. He told me that firing them would be the *worst* thing we could ever do to the company. Of course I asked him why. He looked me dead in the eye and said, 'Because, Len, if you had it your way, you *would* give the company away. Those guys help you keep your balance.' I was so mad at Bill I didn't talk to him for a week!"

"To put it in the language you used yesterday, Simeon, I guess Bill gave you what you needed, not necessarily what you wanted, correct?"

Simeon nodded. "Once I got over my hurt feelings, I realized that Bill was right. Even though Jay, Kenny, and I fought a lot, our final decisions were usually a compromise and pretty well balanced. I needed those guys and they needed me."

"My boss at work, who is becoming smarter with each passing day that I'm here, always cautions me and the other plant managers in our company not to surround ourselves with 'yes' people or people like ourselves. He likes to say, 'In your staff meetings, if all ten of you agree on everything, then nine of you are probably unnecessary.' I think I need to listen to him a bit more."

"He sounds like a wise man, John."

"Yes, I suppose he is. By the way, what did you find out about meeting me for breakfast instead of these early morning chapel sessions?"

"Unfortunately I have a bit of bad news. Last night the abbot came to my room and denied me permission to share meals with you."

"You *really* needed permission to eat with me?" I asked sarcastically, my feelings a little hurt.

"Yes, as I said Sunday morning, the monks share meals in the cloistered section. We need special permission to take our meals elsewhere. I asked Brother James and he denied my request. I'm sure he has a very good reason."

I had met the abbot while walking the grounds during Monday afternoon's break period. To say I wasn't particularly impressed by him would be putting it nicely. He had been elected by the monks to serve as abbot more than two decades earlier, but to me he seemed very old—tired and even a bit senile. And here Len Hoffman had to ask special permission from this feeble old man just to have breakfast with me? And the permission was denied! I just didn't get it. But to be totally honest, I was probably most irritated by the thought of having to get out of bed at this godforsaken hour for another four days.

In a condescending tone I asked, "Please don't take this the wrong way, but don't you think it's a little silly having to ask permission to eat with me?"

"At first I probably did," he replied. "But now I don't give it another thought. Obedience, among other things, has also done wonders for breaking me of my false ego and pride. And those two traits can really get in the way of our growth if we let them."

"I see," I nodded, without a clue as to what he was talking about.

AT THE NINE O'CLOCK CHIME, the principal was waving her hand.

"Yes, Theresa," Simeon responded. "What are you moved to ask this beautiful morning?"

"Last night at dinner we had quite a lively discussion about who was the greatest leader of all time. Many names were suggested but we couldn't seem to come to consensus on one. Simeon, who do you believe was the greatest leader of all time?"

"Jesus Christ," came the matter-of-fact reply.

I looked over and noticed Greg was rolling his eyes and one or two others were also looking uncomfortable.

Theresa continued, "Since you are Christian and have chosen this rather unusual lifestyle for yourself, I guess it would make sense that you believe Jesus was a good leader."

"No, not a good leader, the greatest leader of all time," the teacher reemphasized. "I have come to this conclusion for reasons many of you may not suspect and most of those reasons are very pragmatic."

"Oh, please, let's don't go off on some Jesus tangent," the sergeant broke out. "I didn't come here for that. I came here—no, I got sent here—to learn something about leadership."

"Excuse me, Greg! Why don't you lighten up a bit?" I snapped.

Simeon asked, "Did you like our definition of leadership two days ago, Greg?"

"Yeah, as a matter of fact I did. If you recall, I helped put it together."

"That's right, you did, Greg. We agreed that leadership was the skill of influencing people to work enthusiastically toward goals identified as being for the common good. Is that correct?"

"That's correct."

"Well, I know of no one, living or dead, who even comes close to Jesus in personifying that definition. Let's look at the facts. As I stand here today, over two billion people, fully one-third of the human beings on this planet, call themselves Christian. The second largest world religion, Islam, is less than half the size of Christianity. Two of this country's biggest holidays, Christmas and Easter, are based on events in His life and our calendar even records the years since He lived, now approaching two thousand. I don't care if you're Buddhist, Hindu, atheist, or from the 'Church of What's Happening Now,' no one can deny that this person has influenced billions, today and throughout history. There is not even a close second."

"I see your point. . . ."

"And how would you describe Jesus' management, excuse me, leadership style?" the nurse inquired.

The preacher suddenly exclaimed, "I just had a little revelation here, and I think I'm moved to speak so I better. As I recall, Jesus simply said that to lead you must be willing to serve. I guess you could call it servant leadership. Now remember, Jesus didn't use a power style because He *had* no power. King Herod, Pontius Pilate, the Romans—those folks had all the power. But Jesus had a great deal of influence, what Simeon calls authority, and He is able to influence people even to this day. He never used power, never forced or coerced people into following Him."

"I would rather hear about how you were so successful as a leader," the coach suggested. "How would you describe your leadership style, Simeon?"

"I must confess that it is one I copied from Jesus, but I am happy to share it with you. Freely have I received so freely will I give," he said with a grin.

He walked over to the flip chart and again drew an upside-down triangle divided into five sections. In the top section he wrote "Leadership," saying, "Leadership is where we are going so I will put that at the top of the pyramid. The upside-down pyramid symbolizes the

LEADERSHIP MODEL

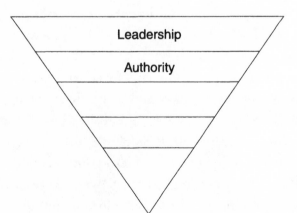

servant leadership model. And, one more time, how do we define leadership, Greg?"

"As a skill," he recited, "of influencing people to work enthusiastically toward goals identified as being for the common good. I know it by heart now."

"Thank you, Greg. Now leadership that is going to go the distance and stand the test of time must be built upon authority," Simeon announced, backing away from the chart.

"As I said the other day," he continued, "you can get a few seasons out of power but over time relationships will deteriorate and so will your influence. Does anyone recall how we defined authority?"

The nurse spoke right up without even consulting her notes. "You said it was the skill of getting people to *willingly* do your will because of your personal influence."

"That's right. Thank you, Kim. So how do we build influence with people? How do we get people to willingly do our will? How do we get people involved and committed from the neck up? What is authority built on?"

"Jesus said influence, leadership, is built on service," the preacher answered. "When we did the exercise yesterday of describing someone in our lives who led us with influence and authority, the person I chose was my first boss and mentor. She truly cared about me and the development of my career, I think even before her own. It's like you said, Simeon. She met my needs even before I knew they were needs. She served me without my even being aware it was happening."

"Thank you for that, Lee, you've nailed it. Authority is always built on service and sacrifice. In fact, I know for certain that if each of you will reflect for a moment on the person you selected in the authority exercise, I'm sure you selected a person who in some way served and sacrificed for you."

I immediately thought about my mother.

"But really, Simeon, in case you haven't noticed, this is a power world," the sergeant insisted. "Can you give us any examples where service, sacrifice, and building influence were really effective at getting things done in the real world?"

"Well, what about Jesus' life," the preacher offered. "He changed the world without ever exercising power, only influence. In fact, I recently preached a sermon on this. Jesus once said, 'I will draw all men to myself if I be lifted up.' He was of course describing His sacrifice of being lifted up on a cross. And He certainly did draw many as a result of this sacrifice."

"Cut the preaching," the sergeant snapped, red-faced. "Don't tell me about a couple of thousand years ago. I asked about the real world."

"Let's look at some examples in this century, then," said the teacher. "Remember that little man over in India? He managed to get a few things done with authority and no power at all."

"Gandhi," the principal remembered. "Talk about having no power! That great man was less than five feet tall and weighed about a hundred pounds! Gandhi found himself living in an oppressed country of about a third of a billion people, a virtual slave nation to the British Empire. Gandhi flatly stated that he would succeed in obtaining independence from England without resorting to violence. Most everyone laughed at him, but he did it."

"So how did he do it?" the sergeant asked.

"Gandhi knew he had to draw the world's attention to India so others could begin to see the injustice of what was happening. He told his followers they would have to sacrifice as they served the cause of freedom, but through their sacrifice they would begin building influence with those watching throughout the world. He told his followers that they would endure pain and suffering in this nonviolent war of civil disobedience, just as there is pain and suffering in all wars. But he was convinced they could not lose. Gandhi personally served and sacrificed a great deal for the cause. He was imprisoned and beaten for his acts of civil disobedience. He went on severe fasts to draw further attention to India's plight. He served and sacrificed for the cause of his country's freedom until the world took notice. Finally, in 1947, not only did the British Empire give India its independence but they welcomed Ghandi in downtown London with a hero's parade. He did it without resorting to guns, violence, or power. He did it through influence."

"And don't forget about Martin Luther King," the coach interjected. "I did my thesis on him in grad school. Not too many people know that King went to India in the late fifties to study Gandhi's methods. What he learned greatly impacted his strategy in the Civil Rights movement in the early sixties."

"I was just a toddler in the early sixties," remarked the nurse, "but I understand that blacks in the South at that time had to sit in the back of the bus, sit in special sections of restaurants if the restaurant would serve them at all, drink out of separate 'colored' drinking fountains, and endure even worse humiliation. I find it so hard to believe this type of discrimination actually existed in this country."

The sergeant said slowly, "And that was a hundred years after the Civil War! Imagine that war, American shooting American. Believe it or not, we lost more Americans in that war than in all our other wars combined."

The nurse added, "Yet all the power, blood, and suffering of that war didn't change the fact a hundred years later that if a white person entered a bus and all the seats were full, a black person had to stand up and go to the back."

Chris continued, "Dr. King recognized he didn't have the power to do anything about it, either. But like Gandhi, King believed that by serving the cause through sacrifice and even suffering he could bring the nation's attention to the injustices that black people were enduring. Some tried to fight power with power. Malcolm X, the Black Panthers, and others. But power begets more power, and when they tried to use power on old Whitey, they discovered Whitey had some power that he could return the favor with. The genius of Dr. King was that he claimed he could achieve Civil Rights for blacks without resorting to violence. Many laughed at him, too."

The principal said, "The road for King was a difficult one. He had countless personal death threats, threats of violence to his family, he spent time in prison for his civil disobedience, and even had his home and his church firebombed."

"And look what Dr. King and the Civil Rights movement were able to get done in a few short years," the coach interjected. "Dr. King became the youngest man ever to win the Nobel Peace Prize. He became *Time* magazine's 'Man of the Year,' the first African American ever to have that distinction. The most wide-sweeping civil rights legislation ever passed, the Civil Rights Act of 1964, became law and is still with us today. The 24th Amendment to the Constitution was ratified, outlawing poll taxes for voting, the Federal Voting Rights Act outlawing literacy testing became the law of the land, and a black man was appointed to the U.S. Supreme Court."

The nurse added, "And blacks didn't have to sit in the back of the bus or drink out of the 'colored' drinking fountain, and they could sit at the lunch counter in restaurants. It's amazing what King accomplished without resorting to power."

After a few moments of silence, the preacher softly remarked, "I just had a thought. Johnny Carson once commented that there was only one person he could never tell a joke about. He said that person was Mother Teresa—the late Mother Teresa of Calcutta—because nobody would ever laugh at a Mother Teresa joke. Now you tell me, why won't anyone laugh at a Mother Teresa joke?"

The coach answered, "I am sure that it has something to do with the enormous amount of influence she developed in this country and around the world."

"And where do you suppose she got all that authority from?" the preacher continued.

"That woman served," the nurse replied simply.

I felt moved to offer, "And think about the affection that sons often have for their mothers. You know, the 'mom can do no wrong' thing. Just insult a man's mother and you'll see what I mean. I would have done anything for my mom when she was alive. As I reflect upon it now, that influence came because Mom earned the right. Mom served."

EVEN BEFORE THE CLOCK began to chime for the afternoon session, the sergeant was at it again. "I understand how influence, authority, is built from serving and perhaps sacrificing for others. But how does this translate into the work world, or even into my home? What am I supposed to do, nail myself to the time clock, go on fasts every day for lunch, look for lepers in my neighborhood, and do a 'sit-in' at City Hall? I'm sorry, but I just don't see how this stuff applies to the real world."

"Thank you for admitting your struggle, Greg," the teacher replied. "If you're struggling, I'm sure others are as well. Before lunch, we discussed some historic instances of authority to dramatize a point. But the good news is that we build authority *any* time we serve and sacrifice for others. Remember, the role of leadership is to serve, that is, to identify and meet legitimate needs. In the process of meeting needs, we will often be called upon to make sacrifices for those we serve."

"You're right, Simeon," the principal agreed, "it just makes sense that authority is built on service and sacrifice. It's simply the Law of the Harvest—what any farmer knows. You reap what you sow. You serve me, I'll serve you. You go to the wall for me, I'll go to the wall for you. I mean, think about it, when someone does us a good turn, don't we feel naturally indebted? There's no rocket science or magic involved here."

The teacher walked up to the board saying, "Does that help, Greg?"

"Let's just keep going and we'll see how it all fits together," came the tart reply.

Simeon pointed to the flip chart.

"In summary, we've said that leadership that is going to go the distance over the long haul must be built on influence or authority. Authority is always built on serving

LEADERSHIP MODEL

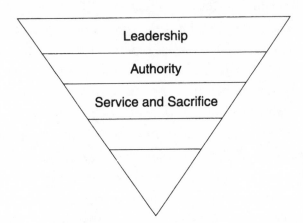

and sacrificing for those you lead, which comes from identifying and meeting legitimate needs. So what would do you suppose service and sacrifice are built on?"

"Effort and lots of it," the preacher volunteered.

"Exactly," Simeon smiled, "But I would like to use the word *love* if that's OK with everyone."

I thought the sergeant might have a coronary right in his chair at the mention of love, but he didn't say a word.

A couple of us were fidgeting nervously so I thought I would ask the question. "I'm sorry, Simeon, but why do you bring a word like *love* into the equation?"

"Yeah," added the coach, "like Tina Turner asks in her song, what's love got to do with it?"

The teacher didn't back down. "The reason we often get uncomfortable about this word, especially in business settings, is because we generally think of love as a feeling. When I talk about love, I am not talking about a feeling. Tomorrow we will be spending a good deal more time discussing this very important word. But for now, suffice it to say that when I use the word *love*, I am referring to a verb describing behavior and not a noun describing feelings."

The principal said, "So perhaps what you're saying is that 'love is as love does'?"

"Beautifully put, Theresa," Simeon acknowledged. "I'm going to steal that one from you and use it later. Love is as love does. That's exactly what I mean."

"And so what is love built on?" the sergeant grunted. "I can hardly wait to hear this one."

The teacher walked back to the board and wrote a simple four-letter word.

WILL

"Love is always built on the will. In fact, I can define this word *will* for you in a formula I learned from Ken Blanchard, the author of that great little classic *The One Minute Manager*. Here's the first half of the formula, are you ready?"

"With bated breath," snorted the sergeant.

Simeon walked to the board and wrote:

INTENTIONS – ACTIONS = SQUAT

"Intentions minus actions equals squat. All the good intentions in the world don't mean a thing if they don't line up with our actions," the teacher explained.

The preacher remarked, "I often tell my parishioners that the road to Hell is paved with good intentions."

Fortunately, the sergeant let that comment go by unchallenged.

The teacher continued, "All my working life, I listened to people tell me how their employees were their most valuable asset. But their actions always spoke their true beliefs. The older I get, the less attention I pay to what people say and the more attention I pay to what people do. People talk a lot alike—but it's often only lip service. It's only in their actions that the differences show up."

"Simeon, I've been thinking," the coach began, "we're up here on the mountain today, in nice surroundings, probably about to hold hands and sing a verse or two of 'Kum Ba Yah.' We're talking theory here on the mountain, but soon we'll be back down in the valley where things aren't always so nice and pretty. Applying these principles down there won't be easy."

"Exactly right, Chris," the teacher affirmed. "True leadership is difficult and it takes a lot of effort. I'm sure you would all agree that our intentions are not very meaningful if they do not line up with our actions. That is why 'will' is at the apex of the triangle. Now here is the second half of our formula."

INTENTIONS + ACTIONS = WILL

Simeon continued, "Intentions plus actions equals the will. It is only when our actions are aligned with our intentions that we become congruent people and congruent leaders. Here then is the model for leading with authority."

After a minute or two, the nurse broke the silence. "Let me see if I can summarize what I've learned, Simeon. Leadership begins with the will, which is our unique ability as human beings to align our intentions with our

LEADERSHIP MODEL

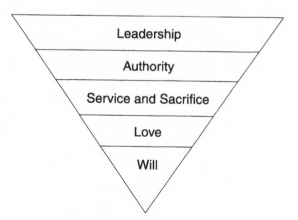

actions and choose our behavior. With the proper will, we can chose to love, the verb, which is about identifying and meeting the legitimate needs, not wants, of those we lead. When we meet the needs of others we will, by definition, be called upon to serve and even sacrifice. When we serve and sacrifice for others, we build authority or influence, the 'Law of the Harvest,' as Theresa said. And when we build authority with people, then we have earned the right to be called leader."

I was amazed at how bright that woman was.

"Thank you for that, Kim," the teacher said. "I absolutely could not have said it better. Who then is the greatest leader? The one who has served the most. Another interesting paradox."

"It seems to me that leadership boils down to a simple four-word job description," the principal commented excitedly. "Identify and meet needs."

Even the sergeant's head was nodding up and down when we adjourned that afternoon.

CHAPTER FOUR

The Verb

I don't necessarily have to like my players and associates but as the leader I must love them. Love is loyalty, love is teamwork, love respects the dignity of the individual. This is the strength of any organization. —VINCE LOMBARDI

IT WAS FOUR O'CLOCK Wednesday morning and I found myself wide awake in my bed staring at the ceiling. Although the week was already half over it seemed like I had just arrived. Much as the sergeant annoyed me, overall I was very impressed with the caliber of my fellow retreat participants and I found the lectures to be engrossing, the grounds beautiful, and the food great.

Most of all I was intrigued by Simeon. He was a master at facilitating group discussion and bringing forth gems of wisdom from each participant. The principles we discussed were simple enough for a child to grasp but profound in ways that kept me awake at night.

Whenever I spoke to Simeon, he seemed to hang on every word, which made me feel valued and important. He was skilled at reading situations, at cutting through the fluff and getting to the core of the matter. He never became defensive when challenged and I was convinced he was the most secure human being I had ever met. I was thankful he didn't push his religion or other beliefs on me, but then again he wasn't passive either. I always knew where he stood on things. He had a disarming and gentle nature, a perpetual smile, and a sparkle in his eyes that communicated a true joy for living.

But what was I supposed to learn from Simeon? My recurring dream continued to nag at me, "Find Simeon and listen to him!" Was there some greater reason or purpose for my being here, as Rachael and Simeon had both suggested? If so, what was that reason?

I had limited time left at this place and I promised myself that I would be more diligent in picking Simeon's brain to see if I could find out.

THE TEACHER WAS SITTING alone in the chapel when I arrived ten minutes early that Wednesday morning. His eyes were closed and he appeared to be meditating so I quietly took a seat next to his. Even sitting in silence with this man did not feel the least bit awkward.

Several minutes passed before he turned to me and said, "What have you been learning here, John?"

Grasping for something to say, the first thing I thought of was, "I was fascinated by your leadership model yesterday. It makes perfect sense to me."

"The ideas and the model are not my own," the teacher corrected me. "I borrowed them from Jesus."

"Yeah, Jesus," I said shifting uncomfortably in my seat. "You might as well know, Simeon, that I'm not much of a religious person."

"Of course you are," he said gently, as if there were no question about it.

"You hardly know me, Simeon. How can you say that?"

"Because everyone has a religion, John. We all have some sort of beliefs about the cause, nature, and purpose of the universe. Our religion is simply our map, our paradigm, our beliefs that answer the difficult existential questions. Questions like, How did the universe come into existence? Is the universe a safe or hostile place? Why am I here? Is the universe random or is there a greater purpose? Is there anything after death? We have all thought about these things, of course some more than others. Even atheists are religious people because they too have answers to these questions."

"I probably don't spend enough time thinking about spiritual things. I've always just gone to the local Lutheran church like my folks did, assuming it was the right thing to do."

"Remember what we said in class, John. All of life is relational, both vertically to God, and horizontally to our neighbor. Each of us has to make choices about those relationships. There is an old saying that 'God has no grandchildren,' and to me that means you do not develop and maintain a relationship with God, or anyone else for that matter, through other people or through hand-me-down dogma or religions. Relationships have to be carefully developed and nurtured if they are to grow and mature. Each of us must make our own choices about what we believe and what those beliefs mean in our lives. Someone once said that everyone has to do their own believing, just like everyone will have to do their own dying."

"But Simeon, how are you supposed to know what to believe? How are you supposed to know what is the truth? There are so many religions and beliefs to choose from."

"If you are truly asking and seeking to find truth, John, I believe you will find what you are looking for."

AT THE END OF NINE CHIMES, the teacher was ready to go. "As I warned you yesterday, our topic today is *love.* I know that may be a little uncomfortable for some of you."

I glanced over at the sergeant, half expecting to witness real-life spontaneous human combustion. No flames or smoke were evident.

After a moment or two of silence, Simeon continued. "Chris asked yesterday, 'What's love got to do with it?' To understand leadership, authority, service, and sacrifice, it is helpful to come to grips with this very important word. I first began to understand the real meaning of love many years ago, while I was still in college. I was a philosophy major at the time and, a few of you may be surprised to learn, a true atheist."

"Now I've heard it all," Greg called out. "Mr. Reborn Monk himself, a nonbeliever? Now how could that be, Brother?"

Laughing, Simeon answered, "Because, Greg, I had studied all the great religions and none of them seemed very plausible to me. Christianity, for example. I really tried to understand what Jesus was trying to say but He kept coming back to this word *love*. He said to 'love your neighbor,' which I figured might be possible provided I had good neighbors. But to make matters even worse, Jesus insisted we 'love our enemies.' To me, this was worse than nonsense. Love Adolph Hitler? Love the Gestapo? Love a serial killer? How can he command people to manufacture an emotion like love? Especially toward unlovable people? To put it in your words, Greg, 'not in this life, big guy!'"

"Now you're preaching, baby!" the sergeant chuckled.

"Then came a turning point for my paradigms about life and love. Several fraternity brothers and I got together one evening for a few beers at the local tavern. One of the language professors, who liked to frequent that same bar, came over to join us and soon the conversation moved to the world's great religions and eventually Christianity came up. I said something like, 'Yeah, love your enemies. What a joke. Like I'm going to have positive regard for an ax murderer!' The professor stopped me dead in my tracks and said I was misinterpreting Jesus' words, although they seemed plain enough to me. He explained that in the English language, we generally associate love with a feeling. You know, I love my house, I love my dog, I love my cigarettes, I love my booze. As long as I have good feelings about something, I can say I love it. We generally do not associate love with anything but positive feelings."

"That's true, Simeon," the principal agreed. "In fact, last night as I was anticipating our topic today, I went to your library here and looked up *love* in the dictionary. There were four definitions and I wrote them down: Number one, strong affection; number two, warm attachment; number three, attraction based upon sexual feelings; and number four, a score of zero in tennis."

"You see what I mean, Theresa? Love is rather narrowly defined in English and most of the definitions involve positive feelings. The language professor explained to me that much of the New Testament was originally written in Greek, one of his language specialties, and he informed me that the Greeks used several different words to describe the multifaceted phenomenon of love. If I remember correctly, one of those words was *eros*, which our English word *erotic* is derived from, and it means feelings based upon sexual attraction, desire, and craving. Another Greek word for love, *storgé*, is affection especially between and toward family members. Neither *eros* nor *storgé* appears in the New Testament writings.

Another Greek word for love was *philos*, or brotherly, reciprocal love. The 'You do good by me and I'll do good by you' kind of conditional love. Philadelphia, the city of brotherly love, comes from this root word. Finally, the Greeks used the noun *agapé* and the corresponding verb *agapaó* to describe a more unconditional love rooted in behavior toward others without regard to their due. It is the love of deliberate *choice*. When Jesus speaks of love in the New Testament the word *agapé* is used, a love of behavior and choice, not a love of feeling."

"As I think of it now," the nurse added, "it does seem a little silly to try to command somebody to have a feeling or emotion for someone else. So he apparently didn't mean we should pretend bad people are not bad when they clearly are or feel good about people who act despicably. But he is saying that we ought to *behave* well toward them. I had never thought of it that way."

The coach jumped in with, "Of course! The feelings of love could perhaps be the language of love or the expression of love but those feelings are not what love *is*. As Theresa put it yesterday, love is as love does."

"Come to think of it," I spoke up, "there are probably . . . no, there are definitely times when my wife does not like me very much. But she hangs in there anyway. She may not *like* me but she continues to *love* me by her actions and her commitment."

"Yeah," the sergeant added surprisingly. "I've heard guys tell me over and over again about how much they love their wives—while they were sitting in bars chasing women. Or parents slobber on and on about how they love their children but can't carve out fifteen minutes a day for them. And some of my Army buddies always tell girls how much they love them when they just want to crawl into the sack. So just saying it or feeling it doesn't make it so, does it?"

"You've got the idea," the teacher said, smiling. "I cannot always control how I *feel* about other people but I certainly am in control of how I *behave* toward other people. Feelings can come and go depending upon what you ate for dinner last night! My neighbor may be difficult and I may not like him very much, but I can still behave lovingly. I can be patient with him, honest and respectful, even though he chooses to behave poorly."

"I think you're losing me here, Brother Simeon," the preacher interjected. "I have always believed, at least my paradigm has been, that when Jesus said to 'love your neighbor,' He was talking about having positive personal regard for them."

"That's just the wimpy Jesus you preachers made up to anesthetize the people," gibed the sergeant. "Like the nurse over there said, how can you command someone to have feelings for someone else? Good *behavior* toward someone, I can buy that, but *feelings* for jerks, that's just a load of B.S."

"Do you always have to be so rude to people?" I practically shouted.

"Just telling it like it is, big guy."

"And generally at someone else's expense," I countered, but Greg just rolled his eyes at me.

The teacher walked over to the flip chart and wrote:

LOVE AND LEADERSHIP

"The New Testament in the Bible gives us a beautiful definition of *agapé* love that illustrates what we're talking about. Your children may have this passage framed on their walls in their bedrooms. It's one of our best sellers here at the Agapé Press. This passage was also a personal favorite of Abraham Lincoln, Thomas Jefferson, and F.D.R. It is almost always read at Christian weddings. Does anyone know what I am referring to?"

"Oh yeah," the coach answered. "That 'love is patient, love is kind' verse, right?"

"Right, Chris," Simeon continued. "First Corinthians, chapter thirteen. It says essentially that love is patient, kind, not puffed up or arrogant, does not behave unbecomingly, does not seek its own, does not take into account a wrong suffered, does not rejoice in unrighteousness but rejoices in the truth, bears all things, endures all things. Love never fails. Does this list of qualities sound familiar to you?"

I remarked, "It sounds a lot like the list of leadership qualities we came up with last Sunday, doesn't it?"

"Rather similar, isn't it, John?" the teacher answered, smiling. "To paraphrase the passage into bullet points, love is: patience, kindness, humility, respectfulness, selflessness, forgiveness, honesty, commitment," Simeon wrote each word on the flip chart. "Now where on this list do you see a feeling?"

"They all look like behaviors to me," the coach replied.

"I submit to you that the beautiful definition of *agapé* love, written nearly two thousand years ago, is also a beautiful definition for leadership today."

"*Agapé* love and leadership are synonymous. Interesting, very interesting," the preacher thought to himself out loud. "You know in the old King James version of the Bible, *agapé* was translated into the English word *charity*. Charity or service better defines *agapé* than the usual English definition of love."

The teacher turned back to the flip chart and wrote out our qualities of character list from the previous Sunday next to the bullet points.

AUTHORITY AND LEADERSHIP	AGAPÉ LOVE
• Honest, trustworthy	• Patience
• Good role model	• Kindness
• Caring	• Humility
• Committed	• Respectfulness
• Good listener	• Selflessness
• Held people accountable	• Forgiveness
• Treated people with respect	• Honesty
• Gave people encouragement	• Commitment
• Positive, enthusiastic attitude	
• Appreciated people	

Simeon continued, "After our break, I would like to ask Theresa to bring in the dictionary from the library so we can better define these behaviors. I think the results may surprise some of you. OK with you?"

"Do we have a choice?" the sergeant asked.

"We *always* have a choice, Greg," the teacher firmly replied.

THE PRINCIPAL HAD THE DICTIONARY wide open on her lap ready to go. "Simeon, I looked up the first word, *patience*, and it talks about 'showing self-control in the face of adversity.'"

The teacher wrote out the definition.

Patience—showing self-control

"God grant me patience and grant it now!" the teacher said with a smile. "Is patience, showing self-control, an important character quality for a leader?"

The coach spoke first, "The leader must model good behavior for the players, kids, employees, or whomever they are leading. If the leader is screaming or otherwise out of control, you sure can't expect the team to be under control or behave responsibly either."

"It's also important," the nurse added, "that you create an environment that is safe for people to make mistakes without worrying about some crazy person going off half-cocked. If you spank a baby who is learning to walk every time she falls, she won't think much about walking, will she? She'll probably decide it's safer to just crawl around, keep her head low, and not take risks. Just like a lot of browbeaten employees I know."

"Oh, I get it," the sergeant smirked. "If my troops screw up I should just speak real nice to them and not get mad. I'm sure I would get a lot done that way."

"I don't think that's what we're saying here at all, Greg," the principal retorted. "The leader has a responsibility to hold people accountable. However, there are several ways to point out deficiencies while allowing people to keep their dignity."

I surprised myself by offering, "Remember, especially in our organizations, that we are dealing with volunteers who also happen to be adults. They are not slaves and they are not animals we're free to beat. Our job as leader is to point out any gaps between the standard that has been set and their performance, but it does not have to be an emotional event. The leader may *choose* to make it an emotional event, but it doesn't have to be that way."

The preacher piggy-backed on my comments with, "The word *discipline* comes from the same root as *disciple*, which means to teach or to train. The goal of any disciplinary action should be to correct or change the behavior, to train the person and not to punish the person. And discipline can be progressive—first warning, second warning, final warning, and finally 'you don't get to be on the team anymore.' John is right, none of those steps needs to be an emotional event."

"Let's move along," suggested the coach. "How is the word *kindness* defined in the dictionary, Theresa?"

Theresa flipped back several pages before answering, "Kindness means 'giving attention, appreciation, and encouragement.'" Simeon wrote it out.

> *Kindness*—giving attention, appreciation, and encouragement

The teacher explained, "Like patience and all the character traits we're discussing, kindness is about how we act, not about how we feel. Let's take the work of attention to begin with. Why would the work of giving attention to others be an important character quality for a leader?"

"Because of what we learned from the Hawthorne Effect," I surprised myself by answering.

"And what, may I ask, is the Hawthorne Effect, John old buddy?" the sergeant quizzed me.

"Best as I can recall, Greg, some Harvard researcher many years ago, I think his name was Mayo, wanted to demonstrate at a Western Electric plant in Hawthorne, New Jersey, that there was a direct and positive correlation between improved worker hygiene and worker productivity. One of the experiments involved simply turning the lights up on the plant floor and sure enough, worker productivity suddenly went up. As they were getting ready to move on to study another facet of worker hygiene, the researchers turned the lights back down so as not to mix up the variables. Guess what happened to worker productivity?"

"It went back down, of course," answered the sergeant, sounding bored.

"No, Greg, worker productivity went up again! So the effect of increased productivity did not come from the cause of the lights going up and down but from somebody paying attention to the people. It's become known as the Hawthorne Effect."

"Thank you for sharing that, John," the teacher acknowledged. "I'd forgotten that story. Paying attention to people was what was important. And I have come to believe that far and away the greatest opportunity we have to pay attention to people is by actively listening to them."

"What exactly do you mean by 'active listening,' Simeon?" the nurse asked.

"Many people wrongly assume that listening is a passive process of being silent while another person speaks. We may even believe that we are good listeners, but what we are often doing is listening selectively, making judgments about what is being said, and thinking of ways to end the conversation or redirect the conversation in ways more pleasing to ourselves."

The principal offered, "Will Rogers once said that if we didn't know it was our turn to speak next, nobody would listen!"

Simeon nodded with a smile. "We can all think roughly four times faster than others can speak. Consequently, there is generally a lot of noise—internal conversation—going on up in our heads as we're listening."

I had to admit that as Simeon was saying these words my mind was back at home thinking of what Rachael might be doing.

"The work of active listening takes place up in your head," he continued. "Active listening requires a disciplined effort to silence all that internal conversation while we're attempting to listen to another human being. It requires a sacrifice, an extension of ourselves, to block out the noise and truly enter another person's world— even for a few minutes. Active listening is attempting to see things as the speaker sees them and attempting to feel things as the speaker feels them. This identification with the speaker is referred to as empathy and requires a great deal of effort."

The nurse added, "At the birth center, we refer to empathy as being *fully present* with the patient. And by being fully present, we don't just mean physically but mentally and emotionally as well. It's not easy to do, especially when there are so many distractions tugging at you. It's a gift of respect to be fully present with someone who is giving birth, to actively listen and anticipate her needs. In my early days as a maternity nurse, I would often be there physically but I was psychologically miles away. When we are fully present, I think that the patients, often on many different levels, sense the difference and appreciate the effort."

The principal nodded and said, "You know, there are essentially four ways we communicate with other people—reading, writing, speaking, and listening. Statistics show that when it comes to communicating, the average person spends roughly 65 percent of the time listening, 20 percent speaking, 9 percent reading, and 6 percent writing. Meanwhile, our schools do well enough at teaching reading and writing, and perhaps they even offer a speech elective or two—but they make virtually no effort whatsoever to teach the skills of listening. And those are the skills the kids will need to use most."

"Interesting, Theresa. Thank you." Simeon went on, "And what are the conscious or unconscious messages we send to people when we extend ourselves by actively listening to them?"

The nurse replied, "The fact that you are willing to set aside all distractions, even mental distractions, sends a very powerful message to the speaker that you *care.* That he or she is an important person. You're right, Simeon, listening is probably our greatest opportunity to give attention to others on a daily basis and convey how much we value them."

The principal added, "Early in my career I used to believe my job was to solve every teacher's or student's problem when they came to me. Over the years I have learned that just listening and sharing the problem with the other person eases their burden. There is a cathartic effect in being listened to and being allowed to express feelings with another person. On the wall in my office at school I have a quote from an old Egyptian pharaoh named Ptahhotep that says, 'Those who must listen to the pleas and cries of their people should do so patiently. Because the people want attention to what they say even more than the accomplishing for which they came.'"

The teacher smiled approvingly. "Paying attention to people is a legitimate human need and one we must not neglect as leaders. Remember, the role of the leader is to identify and meet legitimate needs. I can still recall what my mother told me the day I married my beautiful wife Rita, God rest her soul, fifty years ago this month. She told me never to ignore a woman. Not heeding that advice with Rita got me in hot water more than once! One of the primary works of love is paying attention to people."

"Now that I think about it," I began, "when we had our union drive back at the plant I was told repeatedly that the employees felt like we had forgotten about them, that we weren't paying attention to them as we had in earlier years. On the other hand, the union was sure paying a lot of attention to them during the campaign and the employees were eating it up. I guess people will find a way to get their needs met."

"Thank you for sharing your comments, all of you," the teacher responded. "Now back to our definition of kindness. Theresa read to us that kindness was giving attention, appreciation, and encouragement to others. Do you believe people have a need for appreciation and encouragement, or is that just a want?"

The sergeant snapped, "I don't need any of that appreciation jazz. Just tell me the job to be done and it'll get done. It's the same way I lead my troops because that's what they signed up to do and what they're paid to do. Why on earth should I have to do all this warm and fuzzy stuff?"

The preacher answered first. "William James, probably one of the greatest philosophers this country has ever produced, once said that at the core of the human personality is the *need* to be appreciated. I think anyone who would say that he does not have a need to be appreciated would probably lie about other things too."

"Easy, preacher," the sergeant cautioned.

The nurse jumped in with, "Greg, I always thought the military was big on giving out medals and ribbons as a public demonstration of its appreciation for service and accomplishments?"

"A wise general once said," the principal added, "that a man would never *sell* his life to you, but he will *give* it to you for a piece of colored ribbon."

I also spoke up, "Imagine if I said to my wife, 'Honey, I said I loved you when I married you. If that ever changes I'll be sure to get back to you. And by the way, I'll be sure to bring the paycheck home once a week.' Now wouldn't that be a special relationship?"

To my surprise, the sergeant was nodding to each of the comments without a fight.

The nurse volunteered again, "One of the mentors in my life was my first charge nurse in Labor and Delivery nearly twenty years ago. She once confided in me that she liked to picture in her mind's eye that every employee was wearing one of those sandwich billboard signs. On the front side, the sign would read 'Appreciate Me' and on the back side 'Make Me Feel Important.' That woman had great authority with people. I just didn't know what to call it at the time."

The teacher marched on. "Kindness, one of the labors of love, can be expressed regardless of your feelings for someone. Again, love is not how we *feel* about others, rather how we *behave* toward others. Let me read to you what George Washington Carver had to say about kindness. He said, 'Be kind to others. How far you go in life depends upon your being tender with the young, compassionate with the aged, sympathetic with the striving, tolerant of the weak and the strong. Because someday in your life, you will have been all of these.'"

The coach said, "I think that it's also important to give praise to people. Catch them doing something right instead of being like the 'seagull manager' and constantly looking to catch people doing something wrong."

"You know the old saying, we find what we're looking for," the preacher offered up. "And it's so true. Psychologists call it 'selective perception.' For example, my wife and I began looking for a minivan after we had a child and I became interested in Ford Windstars. Prior to looking for one to buy, I had never really noticed them on the road. Once I became interested, however, I began to see them everywhere! I thought it was a conspiracy or something. I think the same is true with being the leader. Once you begin looking for the good in others, watching out for people doing things right, suddenly you begin to see things you've never seen before."

The teacher added, "Receiving praise is a legitimate human need and is essential to healthy relationships. However, there are two important things to remember about praising people. One, is that the praise must be sincere. Two, it must be specific. Just walking into the department and saying 'Everyone did a great job' is insufficient and may even cause resentment because perhaps everyone *didn't* do a great job. It is important to be sincere and specific by saying, 'Joe, I appreciate the fact that you produced two hundred and fifty pieces last night. Great effort.' You want to reinforce the specific behavior because what gets reinforced gets repeated."

"Let's look at the third word in our love definition, *humility*," the principal suggested, leafing through the dictionary on her lap. "Humility is defined as 'being authentic, without pretense, not arrogant or boastful.'"

> *Humility*—being authentic and without pretense or arrogance

The principal asked, "How is this important for a leader, Simeon? Most leaders I know are very egotistical and full of themselves."

"Damn right," the sergeant jumped in. "A leader has got to be in charge, strong, able to kick butt when necessary. I'm sorry, but I just don't buy into that wimpy, humble stuff."

The preacher took him on again with, "The Jewish Torah, which is the first five books of the Old Testament, claims in the book of Numbers that the most humble man who ever lived was Moses. Now remember who Moses was. He was the guy who smashed the Ten Commandments down the mountain in a fit of rage, killed an Egyptian man for hurting a fellow Hebrew, and was constantly arguing and fighting with God. Now does he sound like a wimpy, poor-pitiful-me kind of man to you, Greg?"

"What's your point, preacher?" he replied sarcastically.

Mercifully the coach interjected, "I think what we want from our leaders is authenticity, the ability to be real with people—we don't want them puffed up and stuck on themselves. Egos can really get in the way and become barriers with people. Know-it-alls and arrogant leaders are a real turn-off for most people. Such arrogance is also a dishonest pretense because nobody knows it all or has it all together. Humility to me is not thinking less of yourself, it's thinking about yourself less."

"We need each other," the nurse said quietly. "Arrogance and pride pretend we don't. The 'lie' of rugged individualism that is so prevalent in this country creates an illusion that we are not and should not be dependent upon other people. What a joke! Another set of hands pulled me from my mother's womb at birth; another set of hands changed my diapers, fed me, nourished me; another set of hands taught me to read and write. Now another set of hands grows my food, delivers my mail, collects my garbage, provides my electricity, protects my city, defends my nation; another set of hands will comfort and care for me when I become sick and old; in the end, another set of hands will lower me into the ground when I die."

The teacher leafed through his notes and said, "An anonymous spiritual teacher once wrote, 'Humbleness is nothing more than a true knowing of yourself and your limitations. Those who see themselves as they truly are would surely be humble indeed.' Humility is about being real and authentic with people and discarding the false masks. What comes next, Theresa?"

"Respectfulness," the principal began reading again. "Respectfulness is defined as 'treating other people like they're important.'"

Respectfulness—treating others as important people

"That's it, now you've lost me for good!" the sergeant said. "I mean, I started getting nervous when you were talking about influence and love. Now you're saying that I have to kiss people's butts with kindness and appreciation and respect. Listen, I'm a butt-kicking drill sergeant and you're asking me to do something that is just not my style. You're asking me to do something that is unnatural for me."

"Greg," Simeon replied quietly, "If I were to bring the top-ranking person in the Army to your base and into your barracks, I imagine you would be very respectful and appreciative; you might even exhibit many of the behaviors we've been discussing. To put it in your terms, I would probably see a lot of 'sucking up' going on, wouldn't I?"

Looking the teacher dead in the eye, the sergeant answered, "You're damn right you would! The general is a very important man and he deserves and will get that respect from me."

"Listen to yourself, Greg!" I said. "You're saying that you know how to be respectful and appreciative, you know how to kiss butt, but you're only willing to do it for those people you see as important. So you're capable of the behaviors but very selective of the recipients for your attention."

The teacher took over from there. "Do you suppose we could treat everyone we lead like a very important person? Imagine treating Chucky on the fork lift like he was the president of the company, or our students like they were school board members, or nurses like they were doctors, or grunts like they were the general. Could you, Greg, treat each member of your platoon like a very important general?"

"Yeah, it's possible, I suppose, but it would be pretty difficult," the sergeant reluctantly conceded.

"That's right, Greg," Simeon continued, "As I keep saying, leadership requires a great deal of effort. Leaders must make the choice about whether or not they are willing to extend themselves for those they lead."

"But I only give people respect when they earn it!" the sergeant continued to object. "After all, respect is earned, isn't it?"

The nurse, in her usual soft and friendly voice, answered, "I'm afraid that old saying might also be a bad paradigm for a leader. I'm a believer that God didn't create human rubbish, only people with behavior problems. And we all have a few behavior problems. But shouldn't someone get 'respect points' just for being a human being? Theresa's definition of respect was 'treating people like they're important.' I think we should add to the end of that definition, 'because they *are* important.' And if you don't buy into that idea, then try out the idea that they should get 'respect points' just for being on your team, in your platoon, your department, your family, your whatever. The leader has a vested interest in the success of those being led. Indeed, one of our roles as leader is to assist them in becoming successful."

That woman continued to amaze me.

Looking at his watch, the Sergeant said, "OK, OK, I get the point but we better get going. We certainly wouldn't want to miss the noon church service, now would we? "

• • •

THE TEACHER RESUMED immediately following the second chime.

"What is the next word in our definition of love, Theresa?"

"First I want to ask you a question, Brother Simeon. Why are the monks so neurotic about time? I mean things are done practically to the second around here."

"I'm pleased you asked, Theresa. Actually, I was a bit of a fanatic about time long before I came to this place. Remember, everything the leader does sends a message. If we are late for appointments, meetings, or other commitments we've made, what is the message we are sending to others?"

"People who are late drive me nuts!" the coach blurted out. "I am actually enjoying the fact that time is respected here because I like to know what to expect. To answer your question, Simeon, I pick up several messages when someone is late. One message is that their time is more important than my time, a rather arrogant message to be sending to me. Being late also conveys the message that I must not be very important to them because they would almost certainly be on time for an important person. It also communicates to me that they are not very honest because honest people stick to their word and follow through with their commitments, even time commitments. Being late is extremely disrespectful behavior and is also habit forming." The coach took a deep breath after her speech. "Thank you for allowing me to preach."

The teacher smiled, saying, "I guess there's nothing more to be said about that. I hope it answered your question, Theresa. Now what is our next definition?"

"Selflessness, but give me a second here to find it. OK, it says selflessness is 'meeting the needs of others, even before your own.'"

Selflessness—meeting the needs of others

"Thank you, Theresa. Now the opposite of selflessness is selfishness, which means 'my needs first, the heck with your needs,' right? Selflessness then is about meeting the needs of others, even if it means sacrificing your own needs and wants. This would also be a beautiful definition of leadership. To meet the needs of others even before your own."

Surprisingly the sergeant offered, "On the battlefield, the troops always eat their meals before the officers."

I found myself protesting this time. "But if we're constantly meeting other people's needs, won't they get spoiled and start to take advantage of us?"

"You haven't been listening too good, John old buddy," the sergeant snickered. "We're supposed to meet needs, not wants. If we're giving people what they legitimately require for their mental or physical well-being, I don't think we have to worry about spoiling them. Remember, John, meet needs not wants, be a servant not a slave. How am I doing, Simeon?"

The class roared as Simeon looked to the principal for the next definition.

"*Forgiveness* is our next word, and it's defined as 'giving up resentment when wronged,'" Theresa announced.

Forgiveness—giving up resentment when wronged

"Now isn't that an interesting definition?" the teacher began. "Giving up resentment when someone has wronged you. Why would this be an important character quality for a leader to develop?"

"Because people aren't perfect and they will let you down," the nurse answered. "And I suppose in the position of being the leader, that will happen quite often."

The sergeant didn't like this one either. "So if someone wrongs me I'm supposed to just pretend they didn't screw up," he said. "I just pat them nicely on the head and tell them everything's OK. Is that right?"

"No, Greg," Simeon countered. "That would not be leading with integrity. Forgiveness is not about pretending bad things didn't happen or not dealing with things as they arise. To the contrary, we must practice assertive behavior with others, not passive doormat behavior or aggressive behavior that violates the rights of others. Assertive behavior is being open, honest, and direct with others but is always done in a respectful manner. Forgiving behavior is dealing with situations as they arise in an assertive manner and then letting go of any lingering resentment. As the leader, if you are not able to let go of the resentment, it will consume you and render you ineffective."

Feeling moved to speak I added, "My wife, whom I lovingly refer to as 'The Shrink,' is a therapist, and she often reminds her patients that resentment destroys the human personality. I think most of us have known people who hang on to resentments year after year and become bitter and very unhappy people."

My roommate threw in, "Buddy Hackett used to say, 'while you're holding a grudge, the other guy's out dancing!'"

"Thank you for all those comments," the teacher smiled. "Remember on Sunday when I said all of us together are much wiser than any one of us? What does the dictionary say about honesty, Theresa."

"Honesty is defined as being 'free from deception.'"

Honesty—being free from deception

"I thought honesty was about not telling lies," the coach said slowly. "But being free from deception is a bit broader, isn't it?"

"We teach our kids in school," the principal offered, "that a lie is any communication with the intent to deceive others. Not speaking up or withholding pieces of the truth may be thought of as 'little white lies' and socially acceptable, but they are lies nonetheless."

"Remember," the teacher continued, "honesty is the quality most people put at the top of their list of what they want most from their leader. We also said trust, which is built by honesty, is the glue that holds relationships together. But honesty with people is also the tough side of love and brings balance to love. Honesty is about clarifying expectations for people, holding people accountable, being willing to give the bad news as well as the good news, giving people feedback, being consistent, predictable, and fair. In short, our behavior must be free from deception and dedicated to the truth at all costs."

My roommate spoke up again. "In my old job in the real world, my first business mentor used to tell me that if we didn't hold our people to task, we were very dishonest. In fact, she used to go so far as to say that leaders who do not hold their people accountable to a set standard are, in effect, thieves and liars. Thieves because they are stealing from the stockholder who pays them to hold people accountable, and liars because they pretend that everything is OK with their people when in fact everything is not OK."

I added, "I've known many a supervisor who thinks that as long as everyone is happy, life in their area is good. They refuse to discuss deficiencies out of fear that they will not be liked—or that people will get angry with them. I never really thought about how dishonest this behavior really is. I think most people want—and they certainly need—to know where they stand with the leader."

"Very good. Let's look at commitment, Theresa," the teacher requested.

"Give me a second. OK, here it is. Commitment is defined as 'sticking to the choice you have made.'"

Commitment—sticking to your choices

The teacher was silent for a moment before saying, "Commitment is probably the most important behavior of all. And by commitment I mean being *committed* to the commitments you make in life. This is important because the principles we are discussing require enormous effort and if you are not committed as the leader, you will probably give up and resort back to power. *Commitment,* unfortunately, is not a very popular word these days."

"I'll say," the nurse spoke up. "If we don't want the baby we abort, if we don't want our spouse we divorce, and now if we don't want Grandpa there's always euthanasia. A nice and tidy throwaway society."

The sergeant smiled before saying, "Yeah, everyone wants to be *involved* but nobody wants to be *committed.* There is a pretty big difference between the two. The next time you're sitting down eating eggs and bacon remember this—the chicken was involved but the pig was committed!"

"Great, Greg—I'd forgotten that one," I jumped in, feeling better about the sergeant the more I got to know him.

All was quiet for some time as we pondered these thoughts. Finally the teacher broke the silence, saying, "True commitment is a vision about individual and group growth along with continuous improvement. The committed leader is dedicated to growing, stretching, and continuously improving—committed to becoming the best leader they can be and that the people they lead deserve. It is also a passion for the people and the team, pushing them to become the best they can be. However, we must never dare to ask the people we lead to become the best they can be, to strive toward continuous improvement, unless we're willing to grow and become the best we can be. This requires commitment, passion, and a vision on the part of the leader of where he or she and the group are headed."

The preacher added, "And scripture teaches us that without a vision, the people perish."

"I wish the mini-sermons would perish, preacherman," the sergeant jabbed at my roommate.

"This love, commitment, leadership, extending yourself for others—this all sounds like a whole lot of work to me," I said with a sigh.

"You bet it is, John," the teacher continued, "but that's what we signed up to do when we signed up to be the leader. Nobody ever said it would be easy. When we choose to love, to extend ourselves for others, we will be required to be patient, kind, humble, respectful, selfless, forgiving, honest, and committed. These behaviors will require us to serve and sacrifice for others. We may have to sacrifice our egos or even our bad moods on a particular day. We may have to sacrifice our desire to blast someone rather than be assertive with them. We will have to sacrifice by loving and extending ourselves for people we may not even like."

"But as you said earlier," Theresa commented, "we have a choice to make about whether or not we will choose to behave lovingly. When we love others by extending ourselves, we will have to serve and sacrifice. When we serve and sacrifice we build authority with people. And when we have built authority with people, then we've earned the right to be called leader."

"I understand the cause and effect of what you're saying," the coach argued, "and may even agree with it. But behaving this way sounds a bit like we're manipulating people."

The principal responded, "Manipulation, by definition, is influencing people for *personal* benefit. I think the leadership model Simeon espouses is influencing people for *mutual* benefit. If I am truly identifying and meeting the legitimate needs of the people I am leading and serving, then they, by definition, must also be benefiting from that influence if I'm serving properly. Is this right, Simeon?"

"As usual, the group has managed to articulate these principles better than I could have. Thank you."

The preacher remarked, "I once listened to a tape done by Tony Campolo, a rather famous author, pastor, speaker, and educator, where he talked about his premarital counseling sessions with young adults. He said that whenever he first sees a young couple, he always asks them, 'So why are you getting married?' The usual answer, of course, is, 'Because we're really in love.' Tony's second question would then be, 'You do have a better reason than that, don't you?' He said the couple would usually look at each other in disbelief at what appears to be a stupid question before answering, 'What could be a better reason than that? We're really in love!' He would respond to this by saying, 'It sounds like you have a lot of warm-fuzzies for each other now and the hormones are really getting cranked up. That's great, enjoy it. But what will become of your relationship when these feelings are gone?' The couple predictably look at one other for strength at that point before responding defiantly, 'That will never happen to us!'"

The room exploded in laughter.

"I see some of you have been married a few seasons," my roommate continued. "We all know that feelings come and go and it is the commitment that carries us through. Tony concludes by pointing out that at every wedding there is an opportunity for a marriage, but that we never know what we've got until the feelings are gone."

"Yes, yes, Lee," the teacher affirmed. "The same principle of commitment is true with leadership. The character traits, behaviors, we have been discussing today are not so difficult with the people we like. Many evil men and women have been kind and outgoing with the people they liked. But our true character as the leader is revealed when we have to extend ourselves for the tough ones, when we are put in the crucible and have to love people we don't particularly like. *Then* we find out about how committed we are. *Then* we find out what kind of leader we've really got."

Theresa added, "I think it was Zsa Zsa Gabor who said that loving twenty men in one year is easy compared to loving one man for twenty years!"

The teacher walked over to the flip chart and completed the diagram.

"In our model yesterday, we said leadership is built upon authority or influence, which is built upon service and sacrifice, which is built upon love. When you lead with authority, you will, by definition, be called upon to extend yourself, love, serve, and even sacrifice for others.

LOVE AND LEADERSHIP

Patience	Showing Self-Control
Kindness	Giving Attention, Appreciation, and Encouragement
Humility	Being Authentic and Without Pretense or Arrogance
Respectfulness	Treating Others as Important People
Selflessness	Meeting the Needs of Others
Forgiveness	Giving Up Resentment when Wronged
Honesty	Being Free from Deception
Commitment	Sticking to Your Choices
Results: Service and Sacrifice	Setting Aside Your Own Wants and Needs; Seeking the Greatest Good for Others

Again, love is not about how you *feel* toward others but how you *behave* toward others."

The nurse summed up with, "So what I'm hearing you say, Simeon, is that *love*—the verb—could be defined as the act or acts of extending yourself for others by identifying and meeting their legitimate needs. Would that be close?"

"Beautiful, Kim," came the simple reply.

CHAPTER FIVE

The Environment

Men and women want to do a good job. If they
are provided the proper environment, they will do so.
—BILL HEWLETT, FOUNDER, HEWLETT-PACKARD

I GLANCED AT THE BEDSIDE CLOCK. It was a little
after three Thursday morning and I was again staring at
the ceiling. I had called Rachael and the office late the
previous afternoon to see how things were going. I was
disappointed to discover that everything and everyone
was getting on just fine without me.

I was also thinking about the life questions Simeon
had posed to me the previous morning. Just what do I
believe? Why am I here? What is my purpose? Is there
any meaning to this game of life?

No answers came to me.

Only more questions.

I ARRIVED AT THE CHAPEL fifteen minutes early and
was proud of myself. I had actually managed to arrive at
a meeting before Simeon!

The teacher sat next to me at five sharp and lowered his head, apparently in prayer.

After a couple of minutes, he turned to me and asked, "What have you been learning, John?"

"The discussion about love was interesting. I never really thought of it as something we do for others. I always thought about love in terms of something we feel. I hope nobody hits me at work when I tell them I'm going to start loving them all!"

Simeon laughed. "Your actions will always speak louder and are infinitely more important than your words, John. Remember Theresa's comment that love is as love does."

"But what about loving myself, Simeon? The pastor at our church says you are also supposed to love your neighbor and yourself."

"Unfortunately, John, that verse seems to get misquoted quite a bit these days. The text actually says, Love your neighbor *as* yourself, not *and* yourself. There is quite a difference. When Jesus says to love others as we love ourselves, He is rightly assuming that we already love ourselves. He is asking us to love others in the same way as we love ourselves."

"The way I love myself?" I objected. "Heck, there are times, especially lately, when I can't stand myself, let alone love myself."

"Remember, John, *agapé* love is a verb describing how we behave, not a noun describing how we feel. There are times when I am not particularly fond of myself, either—

and those are, no doubt, my better moments. Even though I may not particularly like myself at any given time, I still continue to love myself by meeting my own needs. And unfortunately, all too often, I want my needs to come before the needs of others. Just like a two-year-old."

"I guess most of us do tend to look out for number one, don't we?"

"Exactly, John. Looking out for number one is loving ourselves. Putting our neighbors at number one and being mindful of their needs is loving our neighbors. Think of how quick we are to forgive ourselves for the blunders and absurdities that creep into our lives. Are we as quick to forgive our neighbors for their blunders and absurdities? You see, we are quick to love ourselves but not so quick to love others."

"I never thought of it that way, Simeon," I said, a little dumbfounded.

"If we are honest with ourselves, don't we sometimes delight, even for a moment, in our neighbors' misfortunes, job losses, divorces, extramarital affairs, and other troubles? We are truly loving our neighbors when we are as concerned about their welfare as much as we are about our own welfare."

"But what about loving God?" I questioned. "The pastor at my church keeps telling me that I'm supposed to love God too. But there are times I don't feel particularly 'warm and fuzzy' about Him either. Life sometimes seems so unfair. Sometimes I wonder if He's even there at all."

To my surprise the teacher agreed with me. "There are times when I get angry at God and may not like Him very much either. And times when my belief system seems rather implausible to me. I have many questions and there are things in life that appear to me to be unfair. But how I feel has little to do with whether or not I continue to love God and remain committed to my relationship with Him. I can still love Him by being patient, attentive to our relationship through prayer, authentic, respectful, honest, and even forgiving. And I can do this even when, perhaps especially when, I don't feel like it. That is demonstrating the love of commitment. Being faithful, even though my faith may be weak this month."

A few monks were beginning to file in and take their seats.

The teacher's last words that early morning were, "The good news is that when we are committed to love God and others and continue to work at it, positive feelings will eventually flow from positive behaviors, something sociologists call *praxis*. Let's talk about this more tomorrow morning."

EVEN BEFORE THE CLOCK finished chiming, the teacher announced, "Let's switch gears a bit today and talk about the importance of creating a healthy environment for people to grow and thrive. I would like to begin by using the metaphor of planting a garden. Nature clearly shows us the importance of creating a healthy environment if we want growth to occur. Does anyone here do any gardening?"

The coach waved her hand. "I've got a beautiful little garden right behind my condo. I've been gardening for over twenty years—with a real green thumb, if I do say so myself."

"Chris, if I knew nothing whatsoever about gardening, how would you tell me to go about growing a healthy garden?"

"Oh, that's simple. I would tell you to find a piece of land that gets lots of sun and turn over the soil to get it prepared for the planting. Then you would need to plant the seeds, water them, fertilize them, keep the pests away, and weed the garden periodically."

"Now if I do all that you suggest, Chris, what can I expect will happen?"

"Well, in due time you will see some growth and soon the fruit will come."

Simeon pressed further, asking, "When the fruit comes, would it be accurate to say that I caused the growth to occur?"

"Sure," she answered quickly. Then she paused and reconsidered for a moment before adding, "Well, you didn't exactly cause the growth to occur, but you helped it along."

"Exactly," the teacher affirmed. "We don't make things grow in nature. Our Creator is still the only one who knows how a little acorn stuck into the ground one day becomes a large and shady oak tree. About the best we can do is create the proper conditions for growth to occur. This principle is especially true with human beings. Can anyone think of any examples to illustrate this?"

"As a birthing nurse," Kim said, "I can tell you that for a child to develop normally during the nine-month gestation period, a healthy environment within the womb is essential—in fact, conditions must be near perfect. If not, the baby will generally miscarry or some other serious complications may arise."

My roommate jumped in next with, "And once born, I've learned, a child needs a healthy, loving environment to develop properly. I can remember reading about the orphanages created under that dictator in Romania, Nicolae Ceausescu, where babies were literally warehoused with little and sometimes no human contact. Did any of you see the film clips of those babies? Do you know what happens to babies deprived of any human contact?"

"They die," the nurse softly replied.

"That's right, they literally shrivel up and die," the preacher agreed, shaking his head.

After a moment or two the principal said, "I've been working in the public school system for many years and you can pretty well pick out the kids who come from a lousy home environment. Our prisons are filled with people who grew up in sick environments. I'm convinced that proper parenting and creating a healthy home environment are essential to a healthy society. And I am becoming convinced that the answer to crime has very little to do with what happens in the electric chair and much more with what happens in the high chair. When it comes to the importance of creating a healthy environment, I'm with you all the way, Simeon. You're preaching to the choir on this one!"

The nurse added, "This principle is even true in medicine. People sometimes mistakenly believe that they are going to the doctor to be healed. Yet in spite of all the advances in the medical field, no doctor has ever mended a broken bone or caused a wound to heal. The best that medicine and doctors can do is provide assistance in the form of medications and therapies, create the proper conditions, if you will, for the body to heal itself."

"Come to think of it," I jumped in, "my wife, The Shrink, has told me on a number of occasions that therapists do not have the power to heal their patients. She says new therapists often believe they can heal people, but with experience they usually discover they do not possess that power. What a good therapist *can* do is to create a healthy environment for the client by establishing a loving relationship based on respect, trust, acceptance, and commitment. Once a therapeutic and safe environment is created, patients can then begin the process of healing themselves."

"Wonderful, wonderful examples!" the teacher exclaimed. "I hope it's becoming clear that creating a healthy environment is very important for healthy growth to occur, especially with human beings. The garden metaphor is one I have used for as long as I can remember with whatever group that has been entrusted to my care: family, work, military, sports, community, church. To put it simply, I think of my area of influence as a garden that needs tending. As we discussed, gardens need attention and care, so I am constantly asking myself, What does my garden need? Does my garden need to be fertilized with appreciation, recognition, and praise? Does my garden need to be weeded? Do I need to have the pests removed? We all know what happens to a garden if the weeds or pests are allowed to run wild. My garden needs constant attention and I have faith that if I do my part and nurture my garden, I will get healthy fruit."

"And how long does it take before you see the fruit?" the coach asked.

"Unfortunately, Chris, I've known many a leader who has become impatient and given up the effort before the fruit had a chance to grow. Many people want and expect fast results but the fruit only comes when it is ready. And that is exactly why commitment is so important for a leader. Imagine a farmer who tries to 'cram for finals' by planting his crop in late autumn hoping to get a harvest before the snow flies! The Law of the Harvest teaches that the fruit will grow, but we do not always know when the growth will occur."

The nurse remarked, "Another factor in determining when the fruit will ripen is the state of our relational bank accounts."

"What on earth is a relational bank account?" my roommate asked.

"I learned about this metaphor while reading Stephen Covey's best-seller *The Seven Habits of Highly Successful People*. We all know about financial bank accounts where we continually make deposits and withdrawals, hoping never to be overdrawn. The relational account metaphor teaches us the importance of keeping healthy relationship balances with the significant people in our lives, including those we lead. Simply put, when we meet a person for the first time, we basically have a neutral relationship account balance because we don't know one another, we're still kind of testing the waters. As the relationship matures, however, we make deposits and withdrawals in these imaginary accounts based on how we behave. For example, we make deposits into these accounts by being trustworthy and honest, giving people appreciation and recognition, keeping our word, being good listeners, not talking behind other people's backs, using the simple courtesies of hello, please, thank you, I'm sorry, and so on. We make withdrawals by being unkind, discourteous, breaking our promises and commitments, backstabbing others, being poor listeners, being puffed up and arrogant, and so on."

The sergeant said, "So at the afternoon break yesterday, when I called my girlfriend and she hung up on me, that probably means I'm a bit overdrawn, huh?"

"Makes sense to me, Greg!" I laughed. "With our union drive back at the plant we probably had some seriously overdrawn accounts. So what you're saying, Kim, is it may take longer for the fruit to show up depending upon the shape of our relational bank accounts. Is that correct?"

"For those people with whom we have established relationships, I think that would be true. For the new-comers, we generally have a clean slate from which to begin."

"Thank you for another beautiful metaphor that we can use here, Kim," the teacher acknowledged. "This re-lational account idea also illustrates why we should pub-licly praise people and never publicly punish people. Does anyone see why?"

The principal spoke first. "When we publicly punish someone, we obviously have embarrassed them in front of their peers and that is a huge withdrawal out of our account with them. But in addition to that, when you publicly humiliate people, you also make a withdrawal out of your relational accounts with everyone watching because public floggings are horrible to witness and peo-ple wonder, 'When will my turn come?' So I guess if your intent is to make lots of relational withdrawals, publicly punishing people is certainly an efficient way to use your time."

The coach added, "It seems to me that the same prin-ciple would be true when we publicly praise, appreciate, and recognize others. We not only make a deposit into our account with the recipient of the praise, but we also make deposits into the accounts we have with those watching. And as you've said before, Simeon, everyone is always watching what the leader is doing."

"That's right, Chris. Everything the leader does sends a message," Simeon replied. "Somewhere in my office I've got an interesting article and survey that speaks to the high regard people have for themselves and why relational withdrawals are so costly. I'll see if I can dig it up and share it with you after the lunch break."

IT WAS A GORGEOUS AUTUMN AFTERNOON, so I decided to take a little stroll along the sandy cliff running parallel to the beach below. It was sunny, the temperature was in the sixties, and there was a light breeze coming in off the lake. This would ordinarily be my idea of a perfect day but I hardly noticed because my mind was conflicted.

I was excited about the information I was gathering and the prospect of applying the principles when I returned home. At the same time, however, I felt depressed and even embarrassed as I reflected upon my past behavior and how I had been leading those entrusted to my care. What would it be like to have me for a boss? To have me for a husband? To have me for a father? To have me for a coach?

My answers to these questions only served to make me feel worse.

AT TWO, THE TEACHER SAID cheerfully, "I found that article and survey I told you about before lunch. It was in an old issue of *Psychology Today,* and I think you'll find it interesting. The behaviorist who wrote the article says there is not an even correlation between positive and negative feedback. To put it in our 'deposit and withdrawal' terms, he claims that for every withdrawal you take out of your account with a person, it takes four deposits just to get back even. A four-to-one ratio!"

"I can believe that," the preacher responded. "My wife can tell me over and over again how much she loves me, but I can still remember the time last spring when she said I was getting too fat. Now that one really stuck with me!"

"I can see her point though, preacher!" the sergeant jabbed.

"Exactly, Lee," the teacher continued. "We all tend to be pretty sensitive no matter how calm we may try to appear on the surface. To help support this claim, the article goes on to discuss a survey that was conducted to determine how realistically people view themselves. Listen to these numbers. Fully 85 percent of the general public see themselves as 'above average.' Asked about their 'ability to get along with others,' 100 percent put themselves in the top half of the population, 60 percent rate themselves in the top 10 percent, and fully 25 percent rated themselves in the top 1 percent of the population. Asked about their 'leadership ability,' 70 percent rated themselves in the top quartile and only 2 percent rated themselves as below average. And check out the men. When males were asked about their 'athletic ability compared to other males,' 60 percent rated themselves in the top quartile and only 6 percent said they were below average athletically."

"So what's your point?" the sergeant asked.

"The point to me, Greg," the coach jumped in, "is that people generally have a high opinion of themselves. This means we should be very careful about making withdrawals out of others' accounts because they can be very costly."

The teacher added, "Think of building trust in a relationship, for instance. We can spend years of effort building it and it can be lost in an instant of indiscretion."

"You know, here we go again," the sergeant grumbled, his voice rising. "We're talking about all these nice and pretty theories here in this nice and pretty setting, but some of us have to go back and face superiors who are power-oriented and who couldn't care less about authority and upside-down triangles, let alone love, respect, and relational bank accounts. What are you supposed to do if you work for a person like that?"

"Great question, Greg," the teacher said, smiling. "And you are absolutely correct. Power people are generally threatened by authority people, which means it can get uncomfortable. It may even cost us our jobs. There are few places, however, where we cannot treat people with love and respect, in spite of how we are being treated."

"You don't know my boss," the sergeant insisted.

Simeon didn't give up. "When I was working as a business leader, I was often called upon to go into dysfunctional companies and get them turned around. One of the first things I always did in a new assignment was conduct an employee attitude survey to take the pulse of the organization. I would always collate the surveys by department and even by shift to better pinpoint the problem areas. In even the most screwed-up company with terrible survey scores, I would still always find healthy islands of apparent tranquillity in the huge sea of unrest. For example, shipping and receiving third shift, good scores; final end department second shift, good scores; computer room first shift, good scores. When I saw survey scores identifying one of these healthy areas, I would always make it my business to see what was going on in that certain department on that certain shift. And what do you think I would invariably find?"

"A leader," the nurse offered quietly.

"You bet I would, Kim. In spite of the mass chaos, confusion, power politics, and other dysfunctions going on all around, I would find a leader who was taking responsibility for their little area of influence and making a difference. They couldn't control the bigger picture but they could control how they behaved every day toward the people who had been entrusted to their care down there in the bowels of the ship."

"It's funny you should use the analogy of a ship, Simeon," I remarked. "I once had an employee tell me that employees often feel like Charlton Heston in the movie *Ben Hur*. Remember old Charlton Heston, chained to that oar rowing away year after year? He would hear the sounds of hurricanes and ships colliding outside, but they never even let him go up on deck for fresh air or go for a swim in the ocean. And then there was that incessant beating of the drum by the big, sweaty guy to keep the rowing rhythm. Anyway, this employee told me that workers often feel the same way. They're down in the bowels of the ship all day and they never get to go on deck or hear what's going on with the ship. Then the captain yells down that he wants to go waterskiing and the supervisor speeds up the drum beat. And when times are tough, the captain yells down that a few have to be thrown overboard to lighten the ship. Not a pretty picture."

My roommate added, "I have an old coffee mug from my working days that says:

It's not my job to steer the ship;
The horn I'll never blow.
It's not my place to say how far
The ship's allowed to go.
I'm not allowed to go on deck
Or even clang the bell
But if this damn thing starts to sink
Just watch who catches hell!"

"That's great!" I roared. "I need to get one of those mugs! But you know, even if I make the choice to behave in the ways we are discussing, I still have forty supervisory employees who may not buy in. I can't create this environment without their help. How on earth do I get everyone to buy in, Simeon?"

141

"You legislate their behavior," came the teacher's quick reply. "As leader, John, you are responsible for the environment that exists in your area of influence and you have been given power to carry out your responsibilities. Therefore you are empowered to legislate their behavior."

"What do you mean you legislate their behavior?" I objected. "You can't legislate another person's behavior!"

"You sure as hell can!" the sergeant shouted at me. "We do it all the time in the Army, and I'm sure you do it with your people at your plant. You have policies and procedures everyone must follow, don't you? You make them use safety equipment and come to work regularly and follow all sorts of codes of conduct on the job. You and I legislate behavior all the time."

I hated to admit Greg was right, but he obviously had me. If a customer service employee started behaving badly with a customer, their job would be at risk. If employees didn't follow our rules, they quickly became ex-employees. We were constantly legislating behavior as a condition of employment. Suddenly I remembered another example of a company legislating behavior.

"My father," I began, "was a front-line supervisor at the Ford assembly plant in Dearborn for over thirty years. Back in the early seventies, I went to work with him on a Saturday morning and was convinced I would go to college after spending just one hour in that plant. People were screaming, swearing, and carrying on with one another like you wouldn't believe! I mean the place was a jungle. It looked like you got to be the 'Supervisor of the Day' if you could publicly humiliate an employee and simultaneously get at least ten 'F' words into one sentence."

"Sounds like my kind of place," the sergeant called over to me.

"It *was* a special place, Greg," I shot back, realizing he was no longer irritating me. "Anyway, one of my dad's good friends, a fellow supervisor, was unexpectedly transferred to Flat Rock, Michigan, to work in a plant that was part of a joint venture between Mazda and Ford. During his first week on the job as supervisor in that plant, my dad's friend caught an employee doing something wrong and ripped him good and hard in front of everyone on the line. He even managed to get in several 'F' words—your basic Dearborn-style successful disciplinary session! Unfortunately for him, his Japanese manager witnessed the incident and immediately called him into his office. Now remember, the Japanese are big about not 'losing face' in front of others. The manager told my dad's friend very politely and respectfully that he was being issued his one and only warning for this type of behavior. He told him that if he ever witnessed or heard about him publicly behaving that way again, he would be immediately terminated. That very supervisor continued to work in that plant for another decade before retiring. He got the message. I guess you could say, Simeon, that Mazda legislated his behavior."

"Wonderful example, John," the teacher told me. "Everyone should keep in mind, however, that Mazda did not *change* the supervisor's behavior. He changed it himself, because he got the message. We cannot change anyone. Remember the wise saying Alcoholics Anonymous keeps repeating: 'The only person you can change is yourself.'"

The nurse added, "So many people I know *act* as if they can really change other people. They are always trying to fix people, convert them to their religion, get their heads straight, whatever. Tolstoy said everyone wants to change the world but nobody wants to change themselves."

"Isn't that the truth, Kim?" the coach agreed. "If everyone would just sweep in front of their own door, soon the entire street would be clean."

"But, Simeon, as leaders we can motivate people to change, can't we?" the sergeant asked.

"My definition of motivation is any communication that influences choice. As leaders, we can provide the necessary *friction* but people must make their own *choice* to change. Remember the principle of the garden. We do not make the growth occur. The best we can do is provide the right environment and provide the necessary friction so people can choose to change and to grow."

The principal interjected, "Some famous person, whose name escapes me now, once said that there are only two reasons to get married. One is for procreation and the other is for the friction it provides."

"That's a good one," the preacher chuckled. "I know of another place where they legislate behavior. Have any of you ever stayed at a Ritz Carlton Hotel?"

144

"Only a rich preacher like you could afford to stay at a Ritz," the sergeant sneered.

Ignoring the comment my roommate continued, "Once a year I splurge a little and take my wife to a Ritz, which is not too far from our home, for the bed and breakfast special. As soon as you walk into the front door of a Ritz, you know you're in a special place. I mean people **are** practically falling over themselves to meet your needs and there is such an atmosphere of extraordinary respect that it is palpable. Anyway, one evening at the Ritz before dinner, I was sitting in the cocktail lounge sipping a drink—"

"A Baptist preacher sipping a drink at a bar?" the sergeant challenged.

"A virgin daiquiri for my wife and Diet Coke with lime for me, Greg. Anyway, I was watching the two bartenders conduct their business and again witnessed the respect they extended toward the customers and toward their fellow employees. I was intrigued, as usual, so I asked one of the bartenders, 'What is it about you guys?' He answered politely, 'Sir?' 'You know,' I said, 'The way you treat the customers and each another with such respect. How do they get you to do that?' He replied simply, 'Oh, we have a motto here at the Ritz that goes like this: We are ladies and gentlemen serving ladies and gentlemen.' I told him that I thought it was a very catchy phrase but that I didn't understand his point. He looked me dead in the eye and said, 'If we don't behave this way, we don't get to work here! Is there anything about that you don't understand?' I laughed and told him I got his point."

The coach added, "Most of you have heard of Lou Holtz, the famous former Notre Dame football coach. Holtz is renowned for his ability to generate great enthusiasm on the teams he coaches. And not just enthusiasm with the players alone. His entire staff—coaches, secretaries, assistants, even the water boys—are filled with this enthusiasm wherever he has coached in his amazing career. Anyway, the story goes that he was once asked by a reporter, 'How are you able to get everyone to be so enthusiastic on your team?' Lou Holtz replied, 'It's really quite simple. I eliminate the ones who aren't.'"

CHAPTER SIX

The Choice

What we think or what we believe is, in the end,
of little consequence. The only thing of
consequence is what we do. —JOHN RUSKIN

THE TEACHER NODDED "good morning" as he arrived at the chapel Friday morning and seated himself next to me. We sat in silence for several minutes before he asked me his usual question.

"I'm learning so much, Simeon, I don't know where to begin. The idea of legislating behavior with my supervisory team, for example. Now that's a concept I've really got to think through."

"When I was in business, John, I never allowed my personnel people to have extensive employee manuals filled with policies and procedures attempting to legislate the behavior of the masses. I was always much more concerned with the behavior of the leadership team and legislating *their* behavior. If the leadership team is on the right page, the rest will follow naturally."

"That's a good point, Simeon."

"During my career, I would often go into troubled companies and people would be pointing to Chucky driving the fork lift or some gal in shipping and receiving saying that they were the real problem. Nine-and-a-half times out of ten, when I took over a troubled company, the problem was right at the top."

"Funny you should say that, Simeon, because my wife—"

"The Shrink?" laughed Simeon.

"You cut me off," I teased. "That was rather disrespectful of you, sir."

"Please forgive me, John, I couldn't resist."

"I forgive you, Simeon. Anyway, my wife often works with dysfunctional families, and the same dynamic you've experienced seems to occur in her practice. Mom and Dad will bring in children saying, 'Fix these kids! They're acting up all over the place!' Of course, through experience, she knows that the acting up is only a symptom of the real problem. She is now much more concerned with what is going on with Mom and Dad."

"A wise old general once commented that there are no weak platoons, only weak leaders. Do you suppose that union drive at your plant was a symptom, John?"

"Yeah, maybe," I replied, feeling guilty and wanting to change the subject. "Tell me about praxis, Simeon. You mentioned that yesterday morning. You said positive feelings come from positive behaviors. What does that mean exactly?"

"Oh, yes, praxis. Thank you for reminding me. Traditional thinking teaches us that our thoughts and feelings drive our behavior, and, of course, we know this to be true. Our thoughts, feelings, beliefs—our paradigms—do in fact greatly influence our behavior. Praxis teaches that the opposite is also true."

"I'm not sure I follow, Simeon."

"Our behavior also influences our thoughts and our feelings. When we as human beings make a commitment to focus attention, time, effort, and other resources on someone or something, over time, we begin to develop feelings for the object of our attention. Psychologists say we *cathect* the object of our attention or, in other words, we become 'hooked on' or 'attached' to it. Praxis explains why adopted children are loved as much as biological children, why we get so hooked on pets, cigarettes, gardening, booze, cars, golf, collecting stamps, and all the rest of the things that fill our lives. What we pay attention to, spend time with, or serve, we become attached to."

"Hmmm. Maybe that explains why I actually like my next-door neighbor now. At first glance, I thought he was about the creepiest guy I'd ever seen. But over time, as we were forced to work together on a few things around the yard and in the neighborhood, he began to grow on me."

"Praxis also works in the opposite direction, John. During times of war, for example, countries often dehumanize the enemy. We call them 'Krauts,' 'Gooks,'

149

'Charlie' because, over time, dehumanizing them makes it easier for us to justify killing them. Praxis also teaches if we dislike someone and treat them badly, we will come to hate them even more."

"So let me see if I understand this, Simeon. Praxis says if I make a commitment to love and extend myself for those I serve, and align my actions and behaviors to that commitment, positive regard for those people will follow over time?"

"That's basically it, John, 'fake it to make it,' as some would say. A fellow named Jerome Brunner, a noted Harvard psychologist, says we are more likely to act ourselves into a feeling than feel ourselves into action."

"Yeah," I responded. "Too many people, including me, think or say they will behave differently when they feel more like doing so. Unfortunately, many times those feelings never come."

"Tony Campolo, the author Lee mentioned on Wednesday, often speaks about the power of praxis in healing marriages. He claims the loss of romantic feelings that couples often experience before a divorce can actually be corrected if the couple is willing to do the work. To accomplish this, each person makes a thirty-day commitment. They commit to treating their spouse the way they treated them when the great romantic feelings were present, when they were courting. His job is to tell her how beautiful she is, buy her flowers, take her out to dinner, and so on—in short, to do all the things that he did when he was 'in love' with her. She has the same assignment, to treat her husband like a new boyfriend. Tell him how handsome he is, cook his favorite meal, that sort of thing. Campolo claims that for those couples committed enough to go through that difficult assignment, the feelings always return. That's praxis. The feelings will follow the behavior."

"But, Simeon, it's just so hard to get started. Pushing yourself to give appreciation and respect to someone you don't like or to behave in a loving way to an unlovable person is such a stretch."

"Indeed it is. Stretching and growing emotional muscles is much like stretching and growing physical muscles. It is difficult at first. With commitment and proper exercise—practice—however, emotional muscles, like physical muscles, stretch and grow bigger and stronger than you can now imagine."

Simeon just refused to leave me an excuse to hide behind.

I SAT IN THE INSTRUCTION ROOM peering out the window at the beautiful blue lake beyond. The usual fire was roaring in the massive fireplace, snapping and crackling as it burned into a fresh piece of birch wood. It was Friday morning. Where had the week gone?

The teacher patiently waited until the ninth chime before beginning.

"I have known many parents, spouses, coaches, teachers, and other leaders who do not want to assume appropriate responsibility for their role as leader and the choices and behaviors required to be an effective leader. For instance, they will say, 'I will start treating my kids with respect when they start behaving better,' or 'I will extend myself for my wife when she straightens up her act,' or 'I will listen to my husband when he has something interesting to say,' or 'I will extend myself for my employees when I get a raise,' or 'I will treat my people with dignity when my boss starts treating me with dignity.' You've all heard the statement, 'I will change when . . .' and you can fill in the blank. Perhaps the statement should be turned into a question: 'I will change . . . when?'

"I would like to spend our final full day together discussing responsibility and the choices we make. As we discussed on Wednesday, I believe leadership begins with a choice. Some of those choices include facing up to the awesome responsibilities that we volunteered for and aligning our actions with our good intentions. But many people do not want to assume appropriate responsibility in their lives and prefer to lay that responsibility elsewhere."

"Funny you should say that, Simeon," the nurse offered. "Early in my career, I worked a couple of years on a psych floor in a large city hospital. One of the things I quickly discovered was people with psychological problems are oftentimes suffering from 'responsibility' disorders. Neurotics *assume too much* responsibility and believe everything that happens is their fault. 'My husband is a drunk because I'm a bad wife,' or 'My kid smokes pot because I failed as a father,' or 'The weather's bad because I didn't say my prayers this morning.' Character-disordered people, on the other hand, generally *assume too little* responsibility for their actions. They assume that everything that goes wrong is someone else's fault. 'My kid's in trouble at school because of the lousy teachers,' or 'I can't get ahead in my company because my boss doesn't like me,' or 'The reason I'm a drunk is because my father was a drunk.' And then there are those who are in between—character-neurotics—who sometimes assume too much, sometimes too little, responsibility."

"Do you believe we live in a more neurotic or character-disordered society today, Kim?" the teacher inquired.

Before she could answer, the sergeant jumped in. "Are you kidding?" he half shouted. "We have become so character-disordered in America that the entire world is laughing at us! Nobody wants to assume responsibility for anything anymore. Remember the mayor of Washington, D.C., the one who got caught on tape smoking crack and said it was a racist plot? Or how about the woman who drowned her two boys in the back seat of her car and claimed she did it because she was sexually abused as a child? Or the boys out on the west coast who blew their parents away with shotguns and also claimed the 'abuse excuse'? Or the smokers who sue the tobacco companies blaming *them* for their years of chain smoking? Or the 'clairvoyant' who sued a hospital because their CAT scan ruined her psychic abilities and future earning potential? Or how about the disgruntled city worker in San Francisco who shot the mayor and city supervisor and claimed the 'Twinkie defense'? He said he was temporarily insane because he was high on junk food sugar! What's happened to personal responsibility in our society?"

"I believe one of the problems," the teacher continued, "was that we went a little overboard in this country on Sigmund Freud. Although Freud made huge contributions to the field of psychiatry, for which we should be grateful, he planted the seeds of determinism, which has given our society every excuse for poor behavior, allowing us to avoid assuming appropriate responsibility for our actions."

"Could you explain 'determinism,' Simeon?" I asked.

"Taken to its extreme, determinism means that for every effect or event, physical or mental, there is a cause. The cause of following a cake recipe will predictably produce the effect of the cake. At the glass plant where you work, John, the cause of heating up sand, ash, and the other ingredients you use will predictably produce the effect of molten glass. Strict determinism says if we know the causes, physical or mental, we can predict the effect."

"But," the preacher objected, "If we assume cause and effect is true, we arrive at a paradox for the creation of the world, don't we? I mean if we take the universe back to the first split second in time, the fraction of a second preceding the Big Bang, what would explain the first cause? What created that first atom of helium, hydrogen, or whatever? The paradox is that somewhere along the line, something must have come from nothing. And we religious types believe that first cause was God."

The sergeant mumbled, "And you just have to get a sermon in every day don't you, preacher?"

"You're right, Lee, science has never convincingly solved that paradox of first cause," the teacher continued. "But determinism, for every event there is a cause, has generally been believed to be true for all physical events, although even this is being challenged by some of the new science. Freud, however, decided to take it a step further; he applied the same principle to human will. He claimed that human beings essentially do not make choices and that free will is an illusion. He believed that our choices and actions are determined by unconscious forces of which we can never be fully aware. Freud asserted that if we know enough about a person's heredity and environment, we can accurately predict his behavior, right down to the individual choices he will make. His theories dealt the concept of free will a devastating blow."

The principal added, "*Genetic* determinism allows me to blame Grandpa for my lousy genes, which explains why I'm a drunk; *psychic* determinism allows me to blame my unhappy childhood on my parents—which, of course, compels me to make such poor life choices; *environmental* determinism allows me to blame my boss for making the quality of my working life *sooo* miserable, which explains why I behave badly at work! Now I have tons of new excuses for my behavior. Isn't it a beautiful thing?"

"The old nature versus nurture argument," the nurse remarked. "I think we're learning that even though genes and environment have an effect on us, we are still free to make our own choices. Look at identical twins. Same egg, so therefore the same genes—nature. They both grew up in the same home, at the same time—nurture. Yet they are two very different people."

"Or how about those Siamese twins in the recent issue of *Life* magazine. Did any of you see that?" the sergeant asked.

"I believe they refer to them as conjoined twins now, Greg," the preacher corrected him.

"Whatever," he continued. "Anyway, these Siamese twins share the same body, but they have two completely separate heads. But what is really amazing is that the girls have such different personalities, different likes and dislikes, behaviors, and so on. Their parents even said that except for the shared torso, they are two completely different people."

"Again," reiterated the nurse, "same genes, same environment—yet different people."

Simeon continued, "Wonderful examples. I think you will get a kick out of one of my favorite poems, author unknown, which I brought along this morning. It's called 'Determinism Revisited,' and it goes like this:

I went to my psychiatrist—to be psychoanalyzed
Hoping he could tell me why I blackened both my lover's eyes.
He laid me on his downy couch to see what he could find
And this is what he dredged up from my subconscious mind.
When I was one my mummy locked my dolly in a trunk
And so it follows naturally that I am always drunk.
When I was two I saw my daddy kiss the maid one day
And that is why I suffer now from klep-toe-mane-eye-ay.
When I was three I suffered from ambivalence towards my
     brothers
And that is just exactly why I beat up all my lovers!
Now I'm so glad that I have learned these lessons I've been
     taught
That everything I do that's wrong is someone else's fault!
Hey libido, bats in the belfry, jolly Old Sigmund Freud!"

The only one who wasn't laughing was the coach, so I asked, "You don't seem to be buying into this idea, Chris. What's bugging you?"

"I'm not so sure we are free to choose. For example, studies clearly indicate that alcoholics are more likely to have children who are alcoholics. And isn't alcoholism a disease? How can you say that is a choice?"

"Great question, Chris," the teacher replied. "I came from a family troubled by alcohol, and I know I have a certain predisposition to alcohol that I must be very careful about. In fact, back in my late twenties and early thirties, it nearly got the best of me. But even though I may be *predisposed* to a problem with alcohol, does it make sense to place the responsibility for my drinking on my father or my grandfather? *I* am the one who chooses to take that first drink."

Feeling moved to speak I added, "I recently took an executive course on business ethics where they broke up the word *responsibility* into two words—*response* and *ability*. The course taught us that we have all kinds of stimuli coming at us—bills, bad bosses, marriage problems, employee problems, kid problems, neighbor problems, you-name-it problems. The stimulus is always coming at us, but we as human beings have the ability to *choose* our response."

"In fact," the teacher said, speaking more quickly, "the ability to choose our response is one of the glories of being human. Animals respond according to instinct. A bear in Michigan makes the same kind of den as a bear in Montana, and a blue jay in Ohio makes the same kind of nest as a blue jay in Utah. I mean, we can teach Flipper to jump over the wire at Sea World, but Flipper can hardly take credit for the training and may not even be aware of it other than she knows that she will get a belly full of fish at the end of the show."

The sergeant nodded. "Yeah, one guy comes back from Vietnam in a wheelchair, gets addicted to heroin, and burns out, while another comes back from Vietnam in a wheelchair and is head of the entire Veterans Administration. Same stimulus, but I guess a little different response."

The teacher marched on, "Viktor Frankl, I'm sure some of you have heard of him, wrote a famous little book called *Man's Search for Meaning,* and I would highly recommend it to each of you. Frankl was a Jewish psychiatrist who was educated and later became a professor at the prestigious University of Vienna, the same school that educated Sigmund Freud. Frankl became a believer and proponent of determinism, just like his mentor and idol Freud. Then during the war, Frankl was imprisoned in a concentration camp for several years, lost nearly his entire family and personal possessions at the hands of the Nazi regime, and even endured horrible medical experiments upon his body. He suffered terribly and the book is certainly not for someone with a weak stomach. But he learned a great deal about people and human nature in the midst of his suffering, and it forced him to rethink his position on determinism. Let me read to you a section from his book:

> Sigmund Freud once asserted, "Let one attempt to expose a number of the most diverse people uniformly to hunger. With the increase of the imperative urge of hunger, all individual differences will blur and in their stead will appear the uniform expression of the one unstilled urge." Thank heavens, Sigmund Freud was spared knowing the concentration camps from the inside. His subjects lay on a couch designed in the plush style of Victorian culture, not in the filth of Auschwitz. *There,* the "individual differences" did not "blur" but, on the contrary,

people became more different; people unmasked themselves, both the swine and the saints. . . .

Man is ultimately self-determining. What he becomes he has made out of himself. In the concentration camps, for example, in this living laboratory and on this testing ground, we watched and witnessed some of our comrades behave like swine while others behaved like saints. Man has both potentialities within himself; which one is actualized depends on *decisions* but not on *conditions*.

Our generation is realistic, for we have come to know man as he really is. After all, man is that being who invented the gas chambers of Auschwitz; however, he is also that being who entered those gas chambers upright, with the Lord's Prayer or the Shema *Yisrael* on his lips.

After a few moments, the principal quietly stated, "Talk about a paradigm shift! Imagine a full-blooded determinist saying, 'Man is ultimately self-determining, what he has become he had made out of himself,' or, that what is actualized in people 'depends on decisions but not on conditions.' Amazing."

DURING THE AFTERNOON SESSION, Simeon hammered away again on the importance of responsibility and choice.

"I want to tell you a true story that happened to me roughly sixty years ago. I was in the sixth grade and my teacher, Mr. Caimi, uttered what struck me as the most profound words ever spoken. The kids in the class were complaining about having to do homework and Mr. Caimi yelled out, 'I cannot compel you to do your homework!' Now that really got our attention! He continued, 'There are only two things in this life that you *have* to do. You have to die and you have to—'"

"Pay taxes!" the sergeant chimed in.

"Exactly, Greg, die and pay taxes. Now I thought that was the most liberating thing I had ever heard! What a deal for me! I mean, I'm only in the sixth grade so dying is a million years away. And I don't have any money so I can't pay taxes. I'm free at last! So I went home that Tuesday night, garbage night, and my father said, 'Son, please take out the garbage.' I said, 'Hey, wait a minute, Dad. Mr. Caimi taught us today there are only two things in life we have to do, die and pay taxes.' I will never forget his response. He looked at me and said very slowly, but very clearly, 'Son, I'm glad you're learning so many helpful things down there at the schoolhouse. Now you had better grab hold of your butt 'cause you just chose to die!' "

After the laughter subsided, the teacher continued, "But you know, Mr. Caimi didn't tell the truth that day. There are people who choose not to pay taxes. As I speak, there are people up in the forests in the Pacific Northwest who have been living off the land since the Vietnam War. They don't even use money, let alone pay taxes. Folks, there are only two things in life you have to do. You have to die and you have to make choices. From these you cannot escape."

"What if you just decide to drop out of life and not participate in making any choices or decisions?" the sergeant challenged.

The principal answered, "The Danish philosopher Kierkegaard once said that not making a decision is itself a decision. Not making a choice is itself a choice."

"So what's the point of all this choice and responsibility lecture anyway, Simeon?" the sergeant challenged again.

"Remember, Greg, we said the road to authority and leadership begins with the will. The will is the choices we make to align our actions with our intentions. I'm suggesting that, in the end, we all have to make choices about our behavior and accept the responsibility for our choices. Will we choose to be patient or impatient? Kind or unkind? Actively listen or merely be silent waiting for our opportunity to speak? Humble or arrogant? Respectful or rude? Selfless or selfish? Forgiving or resentful? Honest or dishonest? Committed or just involved?"

"You know, Simeon," the sergeant said more quietly, "I've been thinking about my comment to you earlier in the week about how this loving behavior seems unnatural. Lee called me on it and pointed out that I do choose to act that way for important people. But it really doesn't come naturally to me and I get overwhelmed just thinking about trying it with my troops. It just doesn't seem like human nature."

The principal offered another quote. "Human nature—that's 'Going to the bathroom in your pants,' one expert says."

"Well, isn't that special! Where did you get that one?" the sergeant drawled.

"From the author of *The Road Less Traveled*, a psychiatrist and lecturer named M. Scott Peck," Theresa grinned. "It does sound a bit rough on the surface, but I think his point is rather profound. To a young child, potty training seems like the most unnatural thing in the world. It is so much easier to just let it all go in your pants. But in time, this unnatural act soon becomes natural as the child practices self-discipline and develops the habit of using the toilet."

"I suppose that is true of any discipline," the nurse suggested. "Whether it's learning to use the toilet, brushing our teeth, learning to read and write, or virtually any new skill we discipline ourselves to learn. In fact, now that I think about it, discipline is teaching ourselves to do what is *not* natural."

"Wonderful, wonderful," the teacher exclaimed. "We can discipline ourselves to do what is unnatural until it becomes natural and a habit. And we all know we are creatures of habit. Have you noticed you are all sitting in exactly the same spots you started with last Sunday morning?"

"You're right, Simeon," I replied, feeling just a bit silly.

The teacher went on. "Perhaps some of you have learned the four stages of developing new habits or skills. These stages apply to learning good habits as well as bad habits, good skills as well as bad skills, good behavior as well as bad behavior. The good news is that these stages absolutely apply to learning new leadership skills."

Simeon walked over to the flip chart and wrote:

Stage One: Unconscious and Unskilled

"This is the stage where you are oblivious to the behavior or habit. This is before your mother wants you to use the toilet, before you have that first drink or first cigarette, before you learn to ski, play basketball, play the piano, type, read and write, whatever. You are either unaware of or uninterested in learning the skill and are obviously unskilled."

He turned back to the chart and wrote:

Stage Two: Conscious and Unskilled

"This is the stage when you become aware of a new behavior, but have not yet developed the skills. This is when your mother first starts suggesting the toilet; you've had that first cigarette or drink and it tasted so bad; you've put on skis, tried to shoot a basket, sat at the typewriter or the piano for the first time. It's all very awkward, unnatural, and perhaps intimidating. Like you said a minute ago, Greg, right now the thought of applying and practicing these principles is a bit intimidating to you because you are in this stage. But if you stick with it, you will progress to the next stage—" He turned and wrote:

Stage Three: Conscious and Skilled

"This is the stage where you are becoming more and more skilled and comfortable with the new behavior or skill. This is when the child rarely has an accident making it to the bathroom, when the cigarettes and booze are tasting pretty good, when skiing feels a lot less awkward, when someone with the potential of a Michael Jordan is still conscious of his form but he's getting the moves down, the typist and pianist rarely if ever need to look at their fingers on the keyboard anymore. You're 'getting the hang of it' in this stage. What do you suppose would be the final evolution in developing a new habit?"

"Unconscious and skilled," three people spoke out at once.

"Exactly," the teacher said while writing.

Stage Four: Unconscious and Skilled

"This is the stage when you don't have to think about it anymore. This is the stage when brushing your teeth and using the toilet in the morning is the most 'natural' thing in the world. This is the final stage for the alcoholic and the chain smoker, where they are practically oblivious to their behavior, habit. This is when you ski down the mountain feeling as natural as walking down the street. This stage describes Michael Jordan on the basketball court. Many sports writers have quipped that Michael performs as though 'unconscious' on the basketball floor, which is a more accurate description of what is happening than they probably realize. He certainly doesn't have to think about his form or style; it has become natural for him. This stage also fits the highly skilled typists or pianists who are not thinking about individual fingers hitting individual keys. It has become 'natural' for them. Greg, this is the stage where leaders have managed to incorporate their behaviors into their habits and into their very *nature*. These are the leaders who don't have to *try* to be good leaders because they *are* good leaders. A leader in this stage doesn't have to try to be a good person; he is a good person."

"It sounds like you're talking about building character, Simeon," I suggested.

"Exactly, John," he confirmed. "Leadership is not about personality, possessions, or charisma, but all about who you *are* as a person. I used to believe that leadership was about style but now I know that leadership is about *substance*, namely character."

"Yeah, come to think of it," my roommate offered, "many great leaders had very different personalities and styles. Think of the differences between General Patton and General Eisenhower, Vince Lombardi and Tom Landry, Lee Iacocca and Mary Kay, Franklin Roosevelt and Ronald Reagan, or Billy Graham and Dr. Martin Luther King. Very different styles indeed, yet each an effective leader. You're right, Simeon, there must be something more than style and fluff at work here."

Simeon added, "The labors of leadership and love are character issues. Patience, kindness, humility, selflessness, respectfulness, forgiveness, honesty, commitment. These character building blocks, or habits, must be developed and matured if we are to become successful leaders who will stand the test of time."

The principal said, "I hate to lay another quote on you all, but there's an old line about cause and effect that I'm sure the determinists would love, and it seems appropriate here: 'Thoughts become actions, actions become habits, habits become our character, and our character becomes our destiny.'"

"God, I really love that one, Theresa," the preacher asserted.

"Yeah, praise the Lord," the sergeant grumbled, as the session came to a close.

CHAPTER SEVEN

The Payoff

For every disciplined effort,
there is a multiple reward.

—JIM ROHN

I WAS SEATED next to the teacher in total silence at ten minutes before five on our final morning together.

He suddenly turned to me and asked, "What is the single most important thing you have learned this week, John?"

"I'm not sure, but I think 'love,' the verb, has something to do with it," I immediately replied.

"You've learned well, John. A long time ago there was a lawyer, they use to call lawyers scribes, who asked Jesus what the single most important commandment was in Judaism. Now, try to understand the context of this. Judaism had been evolving for centuries and was recorded on thousands of old scrolls, yet this lawyer wanted to know the *single* most important thing in the entire religion! And Jesus obliged him. He told him simply to love God and love his neighbor."

"So love is even more important than going to church or following a certain set of rules?"

"I have found that being supported by a loving community on our journey is certainly helpful but that love is infinitely more important. A wise old Christian named Paul wrote nearly two millennia ago that, in the end, only three things matter: faith, hope, and love. And he said the greatest of these is love. I suspect with love you will be on the right track, John."

"You know, Simeon, you haven't preached at us or imposed your religious belief system on any of us. And you're a monk! At first I was afraid of getting preached at when I came here."

"I think it was Augustine who said we should preach the gospel everywhere we go and use *words* only when necessary."

"Yes, well, I guess you don't really need words. Your life is an example for us all. I mean, you're a model of unselfishness, giving up everything to come here and serve."

"To the contrary, John. There are many selfish reasons I choose to live and serve here. Serving, personal sacrifice, and being obedient to the abbot and the order does wonders for breaking that self-centered nature of mine. The more I break down my pride and ego, the more joy I have in life. John, my joy at times is absolutely indescribable, and I am serving here selfishly seeking more of it!"

"I wish I had a faith like you have, Simeon. But faith, leadership, love, and all the other things we talked about this week are difficult for me and so natural for you."

"Remember, John, things are not always as they appear. Early on I also found these things to be awkward and difficult. The Lord only knows how I struggled and still struggle to this day to deny myself and extend myself for others. But I will admit to you, it is easier now because these things have become more unconscious and skilled. And Jesus helps me along the way."

"Well, I asked for that. I can accept that you believe what you believe and are convinced that Jesus helps you along. But I think I would need a little more proof. Unfortunately for me, you can't prove the existence of God."

"You are right, John. I cannot empirically prove to you the existence of God just as you cannot empirically prove to me that God does not exist. Yet I see evidence of God everywhere I look. You see a different world when you look around. Remember what we talked about earlier, we do not see the world as it is, we see the world as we are."

"Maybe I need to begin looking at things a little differently."

"Remember the power of selective perception, John. We see and find the things we are looking for."

I WAS SITTING on the couch half an hour before the morning session, mesmerized by the fire and completely lost in deep thought. Suddenly, tears began rolling down my cheeks, something I had not experienced in more than thirty years.

171

The sergeant walked over and sat on the couch next to me, patted my knee, and asked, "You OK, partner?"

I just nodded. Strangely, and to my surprise, I was not embarrassed by my tears nor did I feel compelled to cover them up. I just let them flow.

And the sergeant continued to sit right there next to me, in silence.

"THIS IS OUR LAST TWO HOURS together as a group, and I'm curious about any lingering thoughts you may have about what we've discussed. Are there any Yeah-buts? or What-ifs? tugging on anybody this morning?"

"It seems like so much work," I said, my voice cracking a bit. "The effort required to build influence, the work of paying attention, loving, extending oneself for others, and the discipline required to learn new skills and behaviors leaves me with a nagging question, Simeon. Is it really worth all the effort?"

"John, that is a question I have often asked myself over the years. The leader of authority is called upon to make many choices and sacrifices. A great deal of discipline is required. But, of course, that's what we signed up to do when be volunteered to be a leader."

The coach was beginning to squirm in her chair and appeared to be moved to speak. "One of the things we tell our athletes is that discipline requires dedication and hard work, but the good news is that there are always rewards. For example, does anybody here exercise regularly?"

"I try to rollerblade three or four times a week," the nurse volunteered.

Chris continued, "Kim, for the effort and discipline required for you to get out there and rollerblade regularly, would you say that there are multiple rewards?"

"You bet there are!" Kim responded enthusiastically. "I feel better, my mind is clearer, I feel more connected spiritually, I don't have to watch my diet quite as closely, it helps me control my P.M.S.—and that's just for starters!"

"We coaches teach our players that this principle is true with any committed discipline. Think of the multiple rewards of being potty trained, of brushing your teeth regularly, of learning to read and write, of getting educated, of playing the piano, of learning to sew, whatever you learn to do. I would assume the same principle is true with disciplining ourselves to lead from authority."

"You would assume right, Chris," the teacher replied, looking pleased. "There are indeed multiple rewards, or what I like to call 'payoffs.' Can anyone think of any?"

"Well, I'll start with the obvious," the principal replied. "When we choose to extend ourselves by serving and sacrificing for others, we will build influence. A leader who knows how to build influence is a leader whose skills will be in demand."

"Thank you, Theresa. What else?"

"It gives you a mission in life," the sergeant boldly announced.

"What do you mean by that, Greg?" Simeon asked.

"One of the reasons I believe the Army is a good life is that it gives us a mission, a purpose, a vision—a reason to get up in the morning. Like the coach said, there are many payoffs for disciplined effort, including the discipline required to be a military man, er, person. The mission of building authority by serving those for whom the leader is responsible could give that leader a real vision of where he—or she—is headed. And with that vision comes purpose and meaning."

"Beautifully put, Greg. Thank you so much for that gift," the teacher smiled. "As you look at the job description for leading with authority, you can see there is a lot of work to be done. The work of kindness, active listening, giving appreciation, praise, recognition, setting the standard, clarifying expectations, holding people accountable to the standard—this is indeed a daily mission, as Greg said."

"Come to think of it," the preacher added, "a disciplined life of leading with authority amounts to a personal mission statement. It's been popular in recent years for organizations to write their mission statements and articulate what they stand for. But think how important it is to have a personal mission statement of what *we* are about and what we stand for. Someone once said that if we don't stand for something, we will fall for anything."

"One of the things I learned in my corporate life," the teacher interjected, "was that corporate mission statements are fine, and I suppose even serve a useful purpose. But we must never forget that people buy into the leader before they buy into a mission statement. Once they have bought into the leader, they will buy into whatever mission statement the leader's got."

The principal commented, "I am so thankful to you, Greg, for bringing this point up about mission, purpose, and meaning. Our students are searching, sometimes desperately, for purpose and meaning, and if that need is not met, the students turn to gangs, drugs, violence, and a host of other evils to fill the void."

The teacher added, "I once read about a sociological study done on a hundred people over the age of ninety. They asked one simple question on the survey: 'If you were to live your life all over again, what would you do differently?' The three top answers were that they would risk more, they would reflect more, and they would do more that would live on after they were gone."

"Well, this leading with authority sure means taking some risks," the sergeant said without hesitation. "You run into a 'power person' for a boss and you're likely to be on the outside looking in."

"Hey, Greg, all of life is risky," I countered. "Especially for the leader. You know the old saying, the closer you are to the top the closer you are to the door. Bum Phillips, the former head coach of the Houston Oilers, once commented, 'There is only two kinds of coaches, them that's fired and them that's about to be fired!' Face it, the leader is at risk anyway."

"I like the part in the survey about reflecting more," the nurse said quietly. "At the beginning of this week,

Simeon asked us to reflect more on the awesome responsibility of having human beings entrusted to our care. I think those hundred elderly folks are right, we should reflect on our responsibilities today, not in some nursing home in the twilight of our lives."

The preacher added, "I like the part in the survey about doing more that will live on after we're gone. I've spent a great deal of time with the elderly, and this issue of having made a difference in the lives of others is a crucial part of growing old and dying peacefully. In the end, the only important question will be, What difference did our lives make? In our role as the leader, we have a unique opportunity to make a real difference in the lives of others. Or we can just follow the crowd and lead the old-fashioned way, 'Do it or else!' But of course, those who follow the crowd will never be followed by the crowd."

The principal said, "Making a difference in the lives of others is so important. One American Indian tribe has an old saying that goes, 'When you were born you cried and the world rejoiced. Live your life in such a way that when you die the world cries and you rejoice.'"

"I like that, Theresa," the nurse commented. "Simeon, it seems to me that another payoff would be a life of spiritual congruence. If we are truly leading with authority, extending ourselves for others, we will be following the Golden Rule. Our lives will be aligned with God, or our higher power, if you prefer. I took a class on comparative religions several years back and I remember reading

Huston Smith's classic *The Religions of Man.* In the epilogue he discusses the relationships among the world's great religions and concludes that in one very important respect, they are the same. That is, each of the world's great religions contains some version of the Golden Rule."

"Great point, Kim!" the coach exclaimed. "I've always wondered how to integrate my spiritual beliefs with my work and I think I'm getting a clue here. As Vince Lombardi said, we don't have to like our players and associates, but, as leaders, we are called upon to love them and treat them as we would want to be treated. And how do I want to be treated? Do I want my leader to be patient with me, to give me attention, to give me appreciation, to give me encouragement, to be authentic with me, to treat me with respect, to meet my needs when they arise, to forgive me when I screw up, to be honest with me, to give me feedback, to hold me accountable, and ultimately to be committed? You bet I want a leader like that. So the Golden Rule says how I must behave toward those I lead. Just as I would want to be treated."

"If indeed we have a Father in heaven, and of course I am convinced we do," Simeon said gently, "doesn't it make sense that the rule of His house would be to love one another? Again, not love in the sense of how we *feel* about one another, but the manner in which we *behave* toward one another. Let me make an analogy between my being a father of five children and God's situation with His children. As a father, and as much as I would like it to be different, I know my children will not always get along with each other. I know there will be conflict. I know they may not even like one another. But what I do expect is for them to treat one another with respect. To treat one another as the important people each of them are. To treat one another as they would want to be treated, that was the rule in my home. Don't you suppose God looks at His children in a similar way?"

Even the sergeant didn't object to this sermon as we took our morning break.

"WE'RE IN OUR FINAL HOUR together," the teacher began, "and we have discussed multiple rewards for the discipline of leading with authority. But we have left out a very valuable payoff that must be mentioned. And that is the payoff of joy."

"Joy, Simeon?" the sergeant asked—respectfully, for him. "What does being happy have to do with leadership?"

"By joy, Greg, I am not referring to happiness, because happiness is based upon happenings. If good things happen then I'm happy. If bad things happen then I'm unhappy. Joy is a much deeper phenomenon that is not based on outward circumstances. Most of the great leaders of authority have spoken of this joy—the Buddha, Jesus Christ, Gandhi, Martin Luther King, even Mother Teresa. Joy is about inner satisfaction and the conviction of knowing that you are truly aligned with the deep and unchanging principles of life. Serving others breaks you free from the shackles of self and self-absorption that choke out the joy of living."

I was moved to speak. "My wife tells me that she sees plenty of self-absorbed clients who have never grown up emotionally. She has explained it to me this way. In one sense, newborns and infants are the ultimate selfish creatures: virtual 'needs-and-wants machines.' To an infant, personal needs and wants are primary, demanded, screamed for—indeed the infant's very survival is at stake. By the 'terrible twos,' most children practically become tyrants, subordinating the world to their wishes and commands. Unfortunately, many people never grow out of the 'Me first!' stage and go through life as emotional two-year-olds dressed in adult clothing, wanting the world to meet their wants and needs. People who fail to grow up become more and more selfish and self-absorbed. They even build emotional walls around their self-centered lives. My wife tells me that people are terribly lonely and unhappy behind these walls."

The preacher added, "I often tell young people that one of the benefits of the institution of marriage is the way it provides an opportunity for the couple to grow out of their self-centeredness by becoming attentive to the needs of others, namely their spouses. Having children is yet another opportunity to grow and overcome our selfishness as we further extend ourselves for our children. One of the battles of the single life, or even in growing old, is in not becoming overly self-centered. Self-centered people are the loneliest and most joyless people I know."

The nurse spoke again. "It seems as though our ego, pride, and selfishness so often get in the way. In Smith's *Religions of Man* that I mentioned earlier, he states that all of the world's great religions conclude that man's greatest problem since the beginning of time is his self-centered nature, his pride, and his selfishness. Some religions refer to this as sin. Smith concludes that the great religions of the world all teach how to overcome our selfish nature."

The preacher suggested, "My faith teaches that man is born with this curse called original sin. Perhaps our selfish nature is what original sin is all about. Yesterday, we were asking the question, What is human nature? As I thought about that question last night, I realized that my most basic nature is to look out for number one. Extending myself for others is certainly not natural! As Kim said, the discipline of extending ourselves for others is teaching ourselves to do what is not natural."

The principal added, "C. S. Lewis, one of my favorite authors, once said that if you don't believe you are self-centered, then you are probably very self-centered. To dramatize his point he challenges us to look at a set of family snapshots and then ask ourselves, 'Do we or do we not judge the quality of the picture by how *we* look?'"

"Thank you, that's a perfect setup for me," the teacher smiled, nodding. "Loving others, extending ourselves, leading with authority forces us to break down our selfish walls and reach out to other people. When we deny our own needs and wants and extend ourselves for others, we grow. We become less self-absorbed and more 'other' conscious. Joy is a by-product of this extension."

The principal quoted again. "Dr. Karl Menninger, the famous psychiatrist, was once asked what he would recommend if someone were about to have a nervous breakdown. He said he would tell them to leave their house, cross the railroad tracks to find someone in need, and help them."

"I think this is pretty obvious," the sergeant asserted. "When we do somebody a good turn we naturally feel good. Even when I write a check to my favorite charity at the end of the year, I suppose one of the big motivators for me is that it makes me feel good to do it."

"Thank you for your honesty, Greg," the teacher interjected. "I have a quote for you from my one of my favorite people, Dr. Albert Schweitzer. He said, 'I don't know what your destiny will be, but one thing I do know. The only ones among you who will be really happy are those who will have sought and found how to serve.' Perhaps service and sacrifice are the dues we pay for the privilege of living."

The preacher said, "In the book of John, Jesus told His disciples that His incredible joy could be their joy if they obeyed His commandment. He ended by saying, 'This is my commandment, that you love one another, as I have loved you.' Jesus knew there would be joy in loving—the verb—extending ourselves for others."

181

"Please, let's get back to the point before preacher-man starts passing the collection plate!" the sergeant teased, this time with a smile.

The teacher obliged. "The point, Greg, is that there is great joy in leading with authority, which is serving others by meeting their legitimate needs. And it is this joy that will sustain us on our journey through this spiritual boot camp we call planet Earth. I am convinced that our purpose here is not necessarily to be happy or even personally fulfilled. Our purpose here as human beings is to grow toward psychological and spiritual maturity. This is what pleases God. Loving, serving, and extending ourselves for others forces us out of our self-centeredness. Loving others pushes us forward out of our terrible twos. Loving others forces us to grow up."

"And it starts with a choice," the sergeant recalled. "Intentions minus actions equals squat. We've got to act on what we've learned because if nothing changes, nothing changes."

"I may have one better than that, Greg," the principal kidded. "The definition of insanity is continuing to do what you've always done and hoping for different results!"

The group all laughed together.

"Our time together has come to an end," the teacher said, suddenly growing serious. "I have learned a great deal this week and am thankful for the unique gifts and insights each of you brought to our little group."

"Me included?" the sergeant asked in an unbelieving tone.

"Especially you, Greg," Simeon answered sincerely. "In closing, my prayer for each of you is that your journey through life will be adjusted by even a few degrees as the result of having spent this time together. Now a few degrees may not make much of a difference on a short journey, but for the long journey of life it may well put you in a completely different place. Good luck and God bless each of you on your journey ahead."

The Epilogue

*A journey of a thousand miles
begins with a single step.*
—CHINESE PROVERB

THE SIX RETREAT PARTICIPANTS shared a final lunch together before saying good-bye. Tears flowed freely. Even the preacher and the sergeant were hugging each other and laughing out loud.

The sergeant suggested we all meet for a reunion in exactly six months, which we enthusiastically promised to attend. Greg also volunteered to serve as the group's secretary and pledged to keep everyone informed of the meeting date and location. The guy I thought was having the biggest problem with the retreat was the one who didn't want it to end.

It was beginning to dawn on me that the qualities that irritated me most about others, people like the sergeant, were the qualities I disliked most about myself. They were just a bit more transparent in Greg, who was at least honest and authentic about who he was. One of the many resolutions I made that week was to be a little less phony and to work a little more on being authentic with people. "Humility," I think the teacher called it.

"I hope Simeon can join us for our get-together," the nurse suggested. "Make sure you invite him, Greg, OK?"

"Sure thing," the sergeant promised. "But has anyone seen Simeon lately? I was really hoping to say good-bye to him."

I glanced around the grounds for the teacher, but he was nowhere to be seen.

I GRABBED MY BAG from my room and went outside to sit on the bench next to the sandy parking lot. I knew Rachael would be showing up at any moment, and I felt myself getting a little panicky. I just had to say good-bye to Simeon.

I left my bag and walked to the stairway that led down to Lake Michigan. Far below I saw a speck of a man and raced down the stairs yelling, "Simeon, Simeon!" He stopped and turned as I ran to him.

We stood and hugged each other good-bye.

"I don't know how to thank you for this week, Simeon," I stammered awkwardly. "I've learned so many valuable things. I only hope I can apply some of what I've learned when I return home."

The teacher looked deeply into my eyes and said, "Long ago a man named Syrus said that it is of no profit to have *learned* well if you neglect to *do* well. You will do well, John, I'm sure of it."

His eyes communicated to me that he *knew* I would do well, which gave me hope.

"But where do I begin, Simeon?"

"You begin with a choice."

I SLOWLY CLIMBED the 243 stairs and sat back down on the bench next to my bag to wait for Rachael. The last car had just pulled away and the grounds of the monastery were deserted and quiet. I sat listening to the dry leaves rustling together in the warm autumn breeze coming in off the lake. I was soon lost in my thoughts.

I don't know how much time passed before the distant sound of an approaching vehicle brought me back. I could see a trail of dust following our white Mercury Mountaineer as it slowly climbed the two-track trail and turned into the sandy parking lot.

Tears began to well up in my eyes as I slowly got to my feet and looked out over Lake Michigan for the last time. I made a silent resolution.

Hearing the truck door slam, I turned around to see a smiling Rachael running toward me. She looked more beautiful to me at that moment than ever before.

She ran into my arms and I held her close until she let me go.

"What a surprise!" she teased. "I can't remember the last time I let go first. That was kind of nice."

"Just a small first step on a new journey," I replied proudly.

About the Author

Jim Hunter is principal consultant of J. D. Hunter Associates, a labor relations and training consulting firm located near Detroit. He has over twenty years of labor relations experience and is a sought-after public speaker and trainer primarily in the areas of servant leadership and community (team) building. He resides in Michigan with his wife and daughter. He can be reached online at www.jameshunter.com or at (734) 692-1771.